MAKE BOOK CLUB
LIT AGAIN

MAKE BOOK CLUB LIT AGAIN

RECIPES AND IDEAS TO BRING CLASSICS TO LIFE

COLLEEN CONNOLLY-AHERN

NEW DEGREE PRESS

MAKE BOOK CLUB LIT AGAIN

Recipes and Ideas to Bring Classics to Life

ISBN   978-1-63730-670-3   *Paperback*

             978-1-63730-759-5   *Kindle Ebook*

             979-8-88504-044-0   *Ebook*

To my mother,
Maureen Connolly,
who set the alarm clock for midnight, so Mike could
have a hot meal when he got home at 1 a.m.

To my father,
Michael Connolly,
who always ate what Moe was serving up that night.

For all the food prepared, eaten, and shared
with love. Thank you both.

Table of Contents

___

INTRODUCTION   11

PART 1. A LOVE SONG FROM KOREA   17
THE ROMANCE RECOMMENDATION: THE TALE
OF CHUN HYANG   19
THE WORLD OF CHUN HYANG AND LI MONG YONG 25
ESSENTIAL ELEMENTS OF KOREAN CUISINE   31

PART 2. THE TALE OF CHUNHYANG: RECIPES
FOR BOOK CLUB   39
RED MOON MANDU   41
VEGGIE PAJEON   45
SPICY-SOY DIPPING SAUCE   49
ROASTED VEGGIE JAPCHAE SALAD   51
FRUIT (& EGG) SALAD INSPIRED BY CHUN
HYANG'S LOVE SONG   57
TAKE BOOK CLUB TO THE NEXT LEVEL: THE
TALE OF CHUN HYANG   63
ON EATING LIKE A LOCAL IN SEOUL   67

PART 3. A REGENCY ROMANCE RE-READ   71
THE BOOK RECOMMENDATION: PRIDE AND
PREJUDICE   73
THE WORLD OF ELIZABETH AND DARCY   77
ESSENTIALS OF REGENCY ENGLISH CUISINE   81

PART 4. **PRIDE AND PREJUDICE: RECIPES FOR BOOK CLUB** **89**

ZUCCHINI SOUP WITH STILTON   91

VEGAN BLUEBERRY SCONES   95

TEA SANDWICHES   101

A MODEL TRIFLE   111

TAKING BOOK CLUB TO THE NEXT LEVEL:
PRIDE AND PREJUDICE   117

ON CHAMPAGNE, STRAWBERRIES, AND
SHAKESPEARE   121

PART 5. **A TALE WITH A TWIST FROM SPAIN** **127**

THE BOOK RECOMMENDATION: PEPITA JIMÉNEZ   129

THE WORLD OF PEPITA AND DON LUIS   135

ESSENTIAL ELEMENTS OF SPANISH CUISINE   141

PART 6. **PEPITA JIMÉNEZ: RECIPES FOR BOOK CLUB** **147**

TORTILLA ESPAÑOLA   149

PINCHOS DE POLLO Y VEGETALES   155

ROMESCO SAUCE   161

THE "SPANISH" GREEN BEANS   165

ARROZ CON LECHE   169

TAKING BOOK CLUB TO THE NEXT LEVEL:
PEPITA JIMÉNEZ   173

ON CRANKY TODDLERS AND THE KINDNESS
OF STRANGERS IN BARCELONA   177

PART 7. **MARRIAGE AND ROMANCE IN KING
ARTHUR'S COURT** **183**

THE BOOK RECOMMENDATION: EREC AND ENIDE   185

THE WORLD OF EREC AND ENIDE   189

ESSENTIALS OF MEDIEVAL FRENCH CUISINE   195

PART 8. ERIC AND ENIDE: RECIPES FOR BOOK CLUB   **201**

ASPARAGUS WITH A SAVORY EGG SAUCE   203

PORK AND VEGGIE HAND PIES   207

HAND PIE DOUGH   213

HERB AND CHEESE FRITTERS WITH SOUR

FRUIT SAUCE   215

CORNISH GAME HENS WITH GREEN SAUCE   221

SAFFRON BREAD PUDDING   227

TAKING BOOK CLUB TO THE NEXT LEVEL:

EREC AND ENIDE   233

EPILOGUE: THE LITTLE WOMEN CRASH

THE PARTY, OR BETTER UNDERSTANDING

THROUGH BOOKS   237

ACKNOWLEDGEMENTS   245

WORKS REFERENCED   249

Introduction

———

My favorite book, bar none, is *Pride and Prejudice*. I read it
for the first time at St. James Elementary when Mrs. Lyons
suggested it as my second "stretch book," her term for an
above-grade-level read for precocious sixth graders like me.
I spent a lot of time at the dictionary stand that spring, but I
loved the spunky Bennett sisters even better than the March
sisters. This may have something to do with being the only
girl in my family, but sister books still work for me.

I'm not alone in my love of *Pride and Prejudice*. It hasn't been
out of print since 1813; *The Atlantic Magazine* cataloged the
cover of two hundred editions for the novel's two hundredth
birthday in 2013.

Jane Austen's life and her corpus were short—only six completed novels, two of them published posthumously, along
with some unfinished work. But readers couldn't get enough
of her. Realizing what an opportunity that was, the twentieth-century novelist Georgette Heyer created a whole new
literary genre, the Regency Romance, in homage to Austen.
Heyer scrupulously researched nineteenth-century England

for her books, detailing clothing, carriages, and courtly manners so that her books would replicate the culture that Austen was writing about contemporaneously.

Starting in 1935 with *Regency Buck*, Heyer wrote twenty-seven Regencies (and a smaller number of Georgian Romances), deriving her prototypes from Austen's originals. Georgette gave Austen lovers something else to read, varying the situations but sticking to the script: girl meets boy; boy annoys girl; boy finally notices annoyed girl; boy finally manages to win girl. The novels generally ended with an engagement and a very chaste kiss.

That worked fine in the early part of the twentieth century, and there were plenty of authors, such as Clare Darcy and Elizabeth Mansfield (see what they did there with those pseudonyms?), who jumped on the bandwagon. Whole imprints devoted themselves to the genre. But then, the sexual revolution showed up, and the genre felt pretty outdated. It became hard to sell that chaste kiss and earnest proposal to readers raised on *Fear of Flying* and the works of Danielle Steele. Romances changed as well, leaving the Jane Austen parameters behind and bringing steamy sex to the Regency Romance. Anyone who's seen the colossally popular *Bridgerton* series, based on Julia Quinn's novels, has an idea of how far the genre has veered from the original formula.

Yet, love for Jane Austen's masterwork remained. In the late twentieth century, authors started retelling Elizabeth and Darcy's story in ways that made sense to them. They've been sexualized (*Definitely Maybe in Love*), horror-ized (*Pride and Prejudice and Zombies*), neuroticized (*Bridget Jones's Diary*), re-cultured (*Ayesha at Last*), and mystery-ed (*Death Comes to Pemberley*). They've even been comic book-ed (*Manga Classics: Pride and Prejudice*). I've read so many of these re-imaginings that I really couldn't count them all because I love the guilty pleasure of a good—or even a passable—romance novel.

But this Jane Austen lover isn't satisfied. I could never find the one that let me into the main characters' world. I don't want to get between their sheets; I want to get into their kitchens. Every time I read a *Pride and Prejudice* reboot, I keep wondering, "Why hasn't Jane been gourmandized?" In other words, "Where is the food?"

I realized I must think about it a lot when my friends picked up on the trend. My contribution to the Badass Book Bitches' buffet is always designed with our book in mind. Matching the food to the book has become part of the fun of book club meetings for me. I love sharing what I've learned about the history, the customs, and the food with which the characters in a novel would have interacted. Sometimes, it gives insights into the writer and their background work. Sometimes it takes us in a completely unexpected direction. But eating and talking about the food always makes the book discussion better.

I think one reason is the relationship between food and culture. Think about how many first dates involve food. That's because watching peoples' interactions around food helps us evaluate them. Are they generous or cheap? Neat or messy? Classy or lowbrow? Food choices also tell us where people fit into society. Can they get a table at a hot restaurant on late notice? Do they think Five Guys is a good first date? Just like us, Elizabeth and Darcy would have used interactions around food to make decisions about people. But while there are a few specific references to food in *Pride and Prejudice*, they really don't give us much information about how their senses were engaged. And that's a flaw that needs to be addressed. Because understanding their food helps us understand their world. And that brings us even closer to characters we love. And that makes a great book even better.

This collection of recipes is meant to evoke the tastes and aromas that would have accompanied some of world culture's greatest love stories: the *Tale of Chunhyang* from Korea, *Erec and Enide* from medieval France, *Pepita Jimenez* from Spain, and yes, of course, *Pride and Prejudice* from Regency England. For each book recommendation, I've created recipes with the *flavors* of a particular time and a particular place that could easily be cooked by a novice in a decently appointed American apartment kitchen. You don't need fancy, specialized equipment or expensive ingredients. Make one recipe or more—or better yet, dole them out to the members of your book club and share the fun! I've tried to include something for every member of the club in each chapter: the picky eater, the vegetarian, the person who loves sweets, and even the one who prefers to purchase their contribution from the store instead of making it.

Many of these recipes have been inspired by my own travels. As a researcher studying international communications, I have had the chance to travel all over the world and work with incredible people. Diving into the local cuisine highlights every trip—my colleagues are always keen to introduce me to "their" food. Eating in the kind of restaurants that locals love is one of the easiest ways to start to understand a different culture. My hope is that trying these very accessible recipes might spark your curiosity to seek out authentic recipes from masters of the cuisines I pay tribute to here—and I've provided a list of the cookbooks and websites that have inspired my own creations at the end of each chapter. Or maybe they will inspire you to try a new ethnic restaurant. Or read some great translated literature. Or even start your own book club! If this book helps you understand another culture a teeny bit better than you did or step outside your comfort zone, I accomplished one thing I hoped to do.

My other hope for this book is to bring people together. Sure, you could cook any of these recipes on your own, but cooking is so much more fun with a friend. I designed this book with book clubs in mind, but the recipes could also be the basis for a fantastic date night—I've noted movie versions of the books for those who like themed movie nights. Or they could be the center of a fun family evening—kids may not like to talk about what happened in school that day, but they *love* eating history! Talking about the food we're eating and why it's so important to someone's culture opens children's eyes to the world, teaching them things like openness, respect, and empathy. We can never have enough of that.

A LOVE SONG
FROM KOREA

Photo credit: Lee Ahern

The Romance Recommendation: The Tale of Chun Hyang

I'm a sucker for a romance with staying power. And this beautiful Korean *pansori,* or musical story, is one of only five that survive from Korean antiquity. Originally performed by a singer accompanied by a drummer, *Chunhyangga (The Tale of Chun Hyang)* was finally written down by Shin Jae in the nineteenth century. It tells the story of the beautiful daughter of a concubine who catches the eye of the local magistrate's son—a prototypical Cinderella story.

Chun Hyang's early life was difficult. She was the daughter of a *kisaeng,* or courtesan, who was left pregnant and alone when her lover, a local magistrate, was recalled to Seoul. Her mother raised Chun Hyang to be a perfect wife and hostess: she taught her to write, sing, and manage a household. From a cultural perspective, she had many advantages. She was revered in her village for her beauty, her accomplishments, and her virtue. But since her father did not claim her, she was not considered a member of the *yangban*, the scholarly elite that formed the upper ranks of Korea's Confucian society. In contrast, Li Mong Yong, the educated son of the local magistrate, started life with every advantage.

Their story begins on the fifth day of the fifth lunar month, the Spring Festival—when all the young people in the town are celebrating the advent of spring. Chun Hyang, "a flower beginning to bloom," is swinging on a tree swing accompanied by her maid, Hyang Dan, when Li Mong Yong first notices her on a swing under a willow tree. He is immediately captivated and demands she come to him through his servant. But living in a society where women were mostly relegated to the home sphere and standing out in any way was frowned upon, Chun Hyang feared impropriety and ran home. And that, of course, is when it all gets interesting.

Chun Hyang and Li Mong Yong's story takes place during the middle of Korea's Joseon Dynasty (it was mentioned as an "old" story as early as the seventeenth century BCE) and, because of that, gives insight into a society guided by Confucianism. Issues of loyalty, filial piety, and righteousness center the narrative. This is important, seeing as the actions taken by many of the characters in the book wouldn't make sense in a society like ours, driven by very different values; among them, independence, self-actualization, mobility, and progress.

The cultural divide becomes especially clear when Chun Hyang's mother, Wol Mae, brokers a secret marriage contract between Li Mong Yong and Chun Hyang. Wol Mae believes she is securing her daughter's future; although, without an acknowledgment of their marriage by his family, she is putting her daughter in much the same situation that made her own life so difficult. As a modern woman and mother of daughters, I found the scene awful. But it was clear from the text that Wol Mae is a sympathetic character.

The lovers spend a few happy weeks together, but their love is tested when Li Mong Yong's father is recalled to the capital, and his mother sternly refuses to allow him to bring Chun Hyang with him. This leaves Chun Hyang alone and without any protection in a world where a woman alone has little power. That peril becomes clear when the new magistrate sees her and decides he wants her for his own courtesan— and is willing to use unscrupulous means to make it happen. However, it's also clear that her refusal to submit to the magistrate is not what's expected: "To resist the advances of the head man of the area and speak out against him in his own courtyard is an unpardonable crime," says even the royal commissioner who rids Namwon of the evil Pyon. Li Mong Yong is slow to believe in Chun Hyang's innocence. Again, it's difficult for the modern reader to accept his actions, but judging them won't help you understand the characters. It's worth the effort to try and understand the importance of meeting paternal expectations to the abnegation of your personal desires—that's what reading translated literature is all about.

I love to recommend this book because it surprises modern readers. Considering it's a story that's been passed down orally for hundreds of years, written down, and finally translated, *The Tale of Chung Hyang* doesn't feel old, or stiff, or passé. Partly because it focuses so much on human emotion—the feelings of the characters feel so raw and real. Because the text is based on one that was passed on through vocal performance, the language is especially lyrical and descriptive. There are tons of references to contemporary poetry, books, and sights of interest: you get a good idea of just how educated the *yangban* class in Korea was. And for me, one of the best parts of the book is the many references to food and meals and the rituals surrounding them in the culture, which, along with some research into Korean food history, inspired the recipes in this chapter. As a reader, I truly felt like I was getting a peek at daily life in fourteenth-century Korea.

The Tale of Chun Hyang will get your book club talking. How should we analyze the relationship between Chun Hyang and her mother? What about the relationship between Chun Hyang and Li Mong Yong? Is Li Mong Yong truly the hero of this tale?

While not well known in the West, *The Tale of Chun Hyang* would be as familiar to most Koreans as *Pride and Prejudice* is to English speakers. The Korean Cultural Center in the US even offered a virtual performance of the love song from *Chunhyangga* for home-bound audiences during the COVID-19 pandemic. And like many cultural icons, it's been retold and reimagined many times. There are many movie versions available, including the unlikely, light-hearted 1985 musical version *Love, Love, My Love,* which was directed by Shin Sang-ok and his wife Choi Eun-hee while they were being held against their will in North Korea by Kim Jong-Il, who wanted to create a North Korean film industry to rival the one in the South.

Another notable movie version from South Korea was presented at the Asia-Pacific, Cannes, Telluride, and Hawai'i International Film Festivals in 2000. A 2005 mini-series, *Koegeol Chunhyang* (Sassy Girl Chunhyang), was also loosely based on the book. They are available through streaming services, and the over-the-top 1985 version, which apparently included the first kiss in North Korean cinema history, can be streamed for free on YouTube. Any of them would make a fun accompaniment to book club—or a fantastic date night idea, along with some of the recipes in this chapter.

The World of Chun Hyang and Li Mong Yong

———

Chun Hyang and Li Mong Yong's story transports the modern Western reader into a culture defined by the strict social constraints of Neo-Confucianism. *The Tale of Chun Hyang* has existed in written form for less than two hundred years. It was finally written down by Shin Jae-hyo, a pansori theoretician who helped codify the genre and championed the first professional female *pansori* master, Jin Chae-son. But according to most scholars, the *pansori* was performed as early as the seventeenth century, derived from even older folk music. So, it likely describes life in the early-to-middle part of the Joseon Dynasty, which ruled Korea from 1392 to 1910.

Territorially, the Joseon kingdom encompassed the entire Korean peninsula, pretty much the same borders it maintained until the civil war in 1950 divided it into North and South. This, unfortunately, put it smack in between two bigger and more bellicose neighbors: China and Japan. Technically, Korea was part of the Chinese "tribute system," in effect paying its much larger neighbor for protection while maintaining control locally, similar to Europe's feudal kingdoms. Its strategic location led Korea to be occupied by both of its warring neighbors at one time or another, which certainly influenced some aspects of life there. But the Korean language, traditions, and culture are very distinct from its neighbors.

China's influence would have been evident in the country's embrace of Neo-Confucianism, the dominant religious philosophy guiding Korean civil society during Chun Hyang and Li Mong Yong's lifetime. The central focus of Neo-Confucianism is self-improvement, with each member of a society striving to be the best version of themselves in order to achieve transcendence. We see this in Li Mong Yong's attention to his studies and Chun Hyang's devotion to her wedding vows. The religion's focus on benevolence, righteousness, honesty, respect for the state, and respect for family led to a society with strictly prescribed rules of etiquette and social stratification. This is critical because Chun Hyang and Li Mong Yong come from two different classes, which would have made a marriage between them next to impossible: a classic *mésalliance,* as the snarky Bingley sisters would put it.

Li Mong Yong belonged to the *yangban,* or educated gentry class. His father is a successful civil servant and is a royally appointed governor of Namwon. The primary means of advancement of individuals and, consequently, their families was through the passing of governmental exams, or *gwageo.* This led to a culture in which parents were hyper-focused on their children's educations. So, when you hear someone referred to as a "Tiger Mom" or "Tiger Dad," have some respect—you're actually experiencing a social phenomenon that goes all the way back to early Korean culture.

When we first encounter him, Li Mong Yong is studying diligently for the civil service exams, and his mother gently suggests to his stern father that their son might need a break, what with it being Spring Festival and all. The father yields, which sets up the star-crossed lovers' "meet cute" on the tree swing. So, it's an interesting part of the story that the lovers only meet because Li Mong Yong's father bends the rules—I always wonder what the original author of the *pansori* thought of the rigid social system—as, in the end, that's what's often standing in the way of the lovers.

To pass the state exams, young men needed to commit vast amounts of information from the Confucian canon to memory. The emphasis on education is clear from our first encounter with Li Mong Yong, where he discusses features of geography and points of interest he's learned about in books but never actually seen, despite living so close to them. He would also have had to be fluent in Chinese calligraphy, since that was the language all official documents were written in—despite having had a phonetic alphabet, *hangul*, which represented their language perfectly since the mid-fifteenth century. (And before you think that's totally weird, I have a college degree written in Latin hanging in my office, and I can honestly say I have no idea what it says.)

For her part, since her wealthy father's family doesn't acknowledge her, Chun Hyang occupies a lower rung on the social ladder than her lover/husband. Being a courtesan in that society didn't hold the same stigma as it came to in the Western Judeo-Christian societies, so her mother isn't an outcast. In fact, many royal courtesans were quite influential and well-respected. But even though she is virtuous and well-trained, without a man to defend her, she is vulnerable. That vulnerability becomes clear when the new administrator imprisons her when she refuses to become his mistress—there is no independent judiciary to which she can appeal. Chun Hyang wasn't an agrarian laborer, but neither was she a member of the elite. She does not have a substantial dowry to present to her new husband's family. There still weren't a lot of ways of making a living for women outside of marriage. However, in a society with definite barriers between gender and social roles, finding an acceptable match for someone with no clear class was never going to be an easy proposition.

The legality of the "secret marriage" proposed by Chun Hyang's mother, Wolnae, is another problematic plot point. According to Martina Deuchler's *The Confucian Transformation of Korea: A Study of Society and Ideology,* marriage in Neo-Confucian Korea would have been arranged as a contract between families. Women were expected to obey their parents, marry their parents' choice of husband, and become a part of their husband's family. Without the acknowledgment and acceptance of her in-laws, Chun Hyang appears to be in the same situation as her mother was, despite Li Mong Yong's personal written assurance that he will never abandon her.

The Tale of Chun Hyang is THE iconic Korean love story. And yet, it seems that a good deal of its enduring popularity is rooted in its flaunting of traditional Korean cultural values. I love recommending it to book clubs because it's a simple tale that provides so many different areas for discussion. What's the relationship between violating cultural norms and romance? How do child-parental relationships shape the central characters' love story? To what extent does the original musical medium impact the story—so many great places to start a book club discussion.

Essential Elements
of Korean Cuisine

———

The first time you go to a Korean restaurant, it can be pretty overwhelming. There is a LOT going on. When I was in Seoul, my Korean friends did all the ordering, and then I dutifully tasted every little pungent item that came my way, leaving piles of little plates and dishes in their wake. I remember some of it being strange and most of it being delicious. But I couldn't really tell you most of what I ate.

When I wanted to recreate those fantastic flavors at home, I first turned to a classic cookbook, *Growing Up in a Korean Kitchen* by Hi Soo Shin Hepinstall. I found out that despite all that variety, there are basically four main parts to a Korean meal. Cooked rice (*bap*) is the central feature of most traditional meals, and it is where people traditionally get the bulk of their daily calories. Soup (*kuk*) appears at most meals, and it is thought to aid in digestion. Side dishes (*banchan*) add nutrition and pizzazz to the meal. And finally, sauces (jang or yangnyum) fuel the appetite. Fresh vegetables and greens (*namul*) are an optional part of the traditional meal, although they are quite common in summer and for festive occasions.

Korean cuisine, also known as the K-diet in academic and nutritional circles, has become somewhat of a culinary darling lately because of its links to longevity and graceful aging. After all, the average life expectancy for Koreans is more than eighty years old! And while many are familiar with the "French paradox," in which a diet rich in wine and white bread does not seem to lead to high rates of cardiovascular disease (CVD), the Koreans manage even lower rates of CVD than their French counterparts on a diet high in salted foods and white rice. Many researchers believe that what the two paradoxical cuisines may share is the inclusion of a wide range of vegetables, which provide a host of micronutrients and phytochemicals that naturally protect the body. But Korean cuisine is also characterized by a current mainstay of the Superfood Movement: fermented products.

BAP

One way to measure the importance of something to any culture is how many identities it has in the culture. According to food anthropologist Hahm Hanhee, rice has three distinct aspects in Korea. Byeo, the young rice plant, symbolizes Korea's relationship to the gods that gave rice to them. Rice in the field is called *ssal* in Korean, which symbolizes the prosperity and commercial aspects of rice. It's not until it is cooked that it becomes *bap*, which symbolizes the family, who are the people who eat rice made from the same pot. Isn't that a lovely way to define a family? Not surprisingly, for many Koreans, *bap* evokes the same feelings as warm biscuits for many US southerners: hominess and well-being and a sense of togetherness and continuity. While rice is a staple food throughout much of Asia, Korean culture has such a deep relationship with the grain that the word for meal table (*bapsang*) actually includes the word for "rice."

Short-grained white rice is the one you're most likely to see at a Korean restaurant, and it's by far the favorite rice of most Koreans. But with knowledge of the health benefits of fiber in the diet, short-grained brown rice shows up more and more often, both in restaurants and in homes. Short-grained sweet or "glutinous" rice—which actually has no gluten for those avoiding it to worry about—is stickier than regular short-grained rice and is used in rice balls and in some desserts. Before cooking, Koreans usually rinse and soak rice, after which it is either boiled or steamed. If you want to make perfect rice every time, it's probably worth investing in a rice cooker. The best-rated model on Amazon.com is only $23. But if you already own an Instant Pot, you don't need a rice cooker—I find the "Rice" setting makes fantastic, pressure-cooked rice in minutes.

JANG

According to Hooni Kim, Michelin-star chef and author of the wonderful cookbook *My Korea: Traditional Flavors, Modern Recipes*, Korean cuisine depends on three fermented sauces to add umami and spice to most dishes. Because they are fermented, they are tangy and long-lasting. And for the health-conscious, kombucha-drinking set, they're rich in probiotics. And while *jang* is translated as sauce, don't expect the unxiousness of a bernaise or a hollandaise: two of the so-called Korean "mother sauces" are the consistency of pastes, while the other is watery. But like their French compatriots, these sauces help to define the cuisine, providing the umami, smell, and characteristic spiciness of Korean food.

Doenjang and ganjang are actually made together during the process of fermenting soybeans. Doenjang is a thick paste, much stronger and definitely funkier than its Japanese counterpart, miso. The longer it ferments, the darker—and funkier—it gets. That's funky in a good way, like aged cheese. Traditionally a gluten-free food, it's important to note that, like a lot of processed Asian foods, this paste may include cheaper wheat in its formulation. So, if being gluten-free is important to you, you may need to seek out more traditional versions—you can always ask your Korean grocer to help you find one.

Ganjang is the liquid that separates from the paste during the soybean fermentation process that we all know as soy sauce. I have read that ganjang is distinct from Chinese or Japanese soy sauces, but I have to admit I don't remember tasting much of a difference—I guess my palate isn't sophisticated enough. Like doenjang, the best ganjang will be derived from soybeans, not wheat. It will be GF—and it will also be somewhat pricier. For the purposes of the recipes in this book, I recommend you use ganjang or its easier-to-find cousin, tamari soy sauce.

Gojuchang is a slightly sweet and spicy paste ranging in color from fire-engine to brick red. The popular jang is made from red chiles (the heat), rice flour (the sweet), and soy sauce (the salt). I'm going to admit it, I'm obsessed—and I'm not alone.

Always at the vanguard of bringing new trends in cuisine as well as beverages to the masses, *Food and Wine* gave the jang its own feature, "Ketchup's Korean Cousin," by Tina Ujlaki, in 2017. Since then, it's appeared in a host of magazine recipes, in everything from nachos to aioli to cioppino to rimming the glass of their Madame Ae-Ma cocktail. Gojuchang is a fusion darling, gently sparking the palate and making familiar recipes feel somehow new.

KUK

Kuk or *tang*, a brothy soup, is integrated into most Korean meals, along with rice. In a culture that focuses on the function of foods, brothy soup is generally assigned the job of aiding in digestion and in cleansing the palate. According to the popular gastronomy website *Serious Eats*, many Korean soups have particular functions within the culture: hangover cures (*haejangkuk*), cold remedy (*samgyetang*), and even childbirth recovery (*miyeokguk*).

The simplest and most ubiquitous of Korean soups, *doenjangkuk*, is a straightforward mixture of homemade vegetable, kombu, fish, or chicken broth combined with *doenjang*, the fermented soybean paste that is one of the Korean "mother sauces." Doenjangkuk is often brought to the table as an essential part of the meal in a Korean restaurant. Some simple soups, such as those featuring vegetables and seafood, can be ready in minutes. But according to Hi Soo Shin Hempinstall, Korean soups can get far more ornate and use a wide range of ingredients, making the most of long-cooking ingredients such as oxtails and beef knuckles.

BANCHAN

For many—myself included—*banchan*, or side dishes, are the best part of a Korean meal. While rice is comforting and soup is palate-cleansing, neither is exactly exciting. A lot of the spice, sweetness, and earthiness associated with Korean cuisine is in the *banchan*.

Long-lasting, preserved foods are a special class of *banchan* called "*mitbanchan*." Spicy baechu kimchi, made of crunchy Napa cabbage, is the *banchan* most familiar to most Americans. But it turns out "kimchi" is no more synonymous with "cabbage" than "pickle" is with "cucumbers." Kimchi is actually more of a process that involves curing food in a sugar and salt mixture to remove some of the water and then fermenting them in a spicy-sweet gingery marinade. Kimchi-ing vegetables is most common, but Deuki Hong and Matt Rodbard included a recipe for Pineapple Kimchi in *Koreatown: A Cookbook* that will absolutely blow your mind!

You can make kimchi yourself, but you really don't need to— any Korean or Asian grocery store will carry a selection. Like other fermented foods, kimchi's flavor continues to deepen the older it gets. Aged kimchi will be more expensive and far more pungent than younger versions. The *mitbanchan* is so popular that many US grocery stores now stock at least one brand.

THE TALE OF CHUNHYANG: RECIPES FOR BOOK CLUB

"The wine and food are here, young lord."

"Good. Spring and good wine go perfectly together."

Red Moon Mandu

———

My daughter Eleanor LOVES dumplings. When it's her turn to pick the restaurant, odds are dumplings are on the menu. Celebrating passing her driver's license exam? Dumplings. Late-night study snack needed? Dumplings. I'm pretty sure she learned to use chopsticks just so she could look cool while dunking dumplings into the dipping sauce. *Mandu* is Korean for dumpling. And Ellie's my mandu maven.

I have eaten a lot of mandu in Korean restaurants, and I can't really remember one I didn't like. And I've read and followed a few fantastic authentic mandu recipes, including Korean food authority Maangchi's beef and pork version. But with this recipe, I wanted to do something a little different. I wanted to create one easy-to-execute, perfect little bite that would introduce the flavors of Korea to someone who might be new to the cuisine. A big hit of ginger was a given, along with Napa cabbage for texture. But when I added a tablespoon of gojuchang, the dumpling came to life. The sauce also gave them such a lovely red color when they were steamed that Ellie described them as "little red moons." So, this recipe is for her.

Yield: 40–45 small dumplings

Equipment you will need: a steamer basket or vegetable steamer

Equipment that would be nice: a food processor, a salad spinner, a small (2 teaspoon) cookie scoop, a bamboo steamer

Ingredients:

1 medium head of Napa cabbage
2 T chopped ginger (peel ginger skin with a spoon before chopping)
4 cloves garlic
1 lb ground pork or ground turkey
1 T gojuchang (available in many well-stocked grocery stores and any Asian or Korean market)
1 T soy sauce
1 T sesame oil
1 t ground white pepper
1 t Kosher salt
1 egg, lightly beaten
1 egg yolk
1 T water

45 Shanghai-style dumpling wrappers, thawed if frozen

1. Chop the bottom off the cabbage to remove leaves. Thoroughly wash and dry the leaves and reserve a few to line the steamer basket. This will prevent the dumplings from sticking to the bottom of the steamer.

2. Chop the remaining cabbage leaves, measuring 2 cups. (Reserve the rest of the cabbage for another purpose.) Add the chopped cabbage, ginger, and garlic to the bowl of a food processor and pulse to finely shred. Alternatively, you can mince the cabbage, ginger, and garlic together by running your knife over it multiple times. Either way, you want to make sure it's finely chopped. Place the vegetables in a large bowl.

3. Add the ground pork, gojuchang, soy sauce, sesame oil, white pepper, salt, and whole egg to the bowl. Fold together to mix thoroughly, but gently (I use my hands for this, but a large spatula would work).

4. Next, in a small bowl, whisk the egg yolk and water together. One at a time, lay the dumpling wrappers on a plate. Dip your index finger into the egg mixture and spread it around the outer edge of the dumpling wrapper (you want it moist, but not wet). Place 2 teaspoons of the filling in the center of the wrapper. Then, fold the wrapper in half and pinch the edges together to form a half-moon shape, making sure to keep the filling away from the edges. (If you want to get fancy, here's a cool video demonstrating other ways to fold dumplings: https://www.youtube.com/watch?v=hCqf-h95m2A)

5. Place the dumplings in the cabbage-lined steamer basket or bamboo steamer so that they are not touching. Bring water to a boil in the bottom of a pan that you can set your steam tray in. If you have a bamboo steamer, bring water to boil in the bottom of a wok and set the layers of the steamer over it. If you are using a steamer basket, you may have to steam multiple batches. Cover and steam 7–9 minutes, until wrappers are translucent and filling feels firmly set.

6. Serve with spicy soy dipping sauce. Alternatively, you can serve with plain soy sauce or black vinegar instead of whipping up the sauce.

Note: Even if you don't plan to eat 45 dumplings, once you've started the project, it's worth making them all because they freeze really well. Just line a plate or a cookie sheet that will fit in your freezer with parchment paper and place the dumplings in a single layer, making sure they're not touching. Once they are frozen, place them in a freezer bag to store. Cook like a potsticker: Heat 2 tablespoons of neutral oil in a pan with a tight-fitting lid. Add 5 or 6 frozen potstickers and sauté over medium heat until the wrapper is a deep brown, being careful not to burn them. Carefully add a 1/4 cup water to the pan and put the lid on the pan to steam the dumplings until cooked through, 5–7 minutes.

Veggie Pajeon

—

It's a shame that US Americans tend to relegate pancakes to breakfast. Not that I have anything against a fluffy buttermilk stack dripping with maple syrup and butter every once in a while, but once you open pancakes up to the savory side, you gain a whole new perspective on the quickest of quick breads. The French serve up Swiss chard farçous. Colombians dine on arepas. Ashkenazi Jews celebrate with latkes. Apparently, Americans have a lot to learn on the pancake front.

However, in my opinion, it's Korean cuisine that completely ups the savory pancake game, folding vegetables, and sometimes even seafood, into a light batter, frying it up over high heat, and serving it along with a zingy dipping sauce. They come together quickly, and they don't mind hanging around on the plate, so they're a perfect buffet item. And the combination of seltzer and baking powder makes them a little bit fluffy. Kimchi pancakes are a popular Korean restaurant banchan. Chive pancakes are beautiful and traditional. However, I've found what I'm sure most Korean home cooks already know: making pancakes is an easy and inexpensive way to use up the odds and ends I have in my refrigerator. They're also a great way to use up leftover cooked vegetables. In fact, I often throw an extra couple of ears of corn on the grill, just to make the corn version of these in summer! In winter, they're a great way to use up some Brussels sprouts and carrots.

Yield: Two 8-inch pancakes (each cut into eight wedges)

Equipment you will need: an 8- or 9-inch non-stick skillet; two large plates for flipping the pancake

Equipment that would be nice: a pizza cutter; a box grater or food processor if you're shredding vegetables

Ingredients:

Neutral oil, such as canola or grapeseed
6 green onions
3/4 c all-purpose flour
1/4 c potato starch
1/4 t baking powder
8 oz seltzer water
1 1/2 t fish sauce
2 t sesame oil
1 egg yolk
1 1/2 cup shredded or cooked vegetables (such as finely shredded carrots, zucchini or Brussels sprouts, whole corn, or peas, or any combination to make 1 1/2 cups)

1. Trim the root ends and the dark, leafy ends from the green onions, leaving just the white and light green portion.
2. Put the skillet over high heat. Add 1 T oil, swirling the pan to distribute oil. When the pan is very hot (water

will bead up when dropped on it), add the green onions and cook until they are charred on the bottom. Turn them over and char the other side. Remove them from the pan and transfer them to a cutting board. Remove the pan from the heat, and when it's cool enough, wipe it out with a paper towel.

3. Slice the cooled green onions thinly. Set aside.

4. Make the pancake batter: Whisk together the flour, potato starch, and baking powder in a medium bowl. Add the seltzer, fish sauce, sesame oil, and egg yolk, whisking until you reach a somewhat thick batter. Fold in the green onions and the vegetables, making sure they are completely coated.

5. Return the skillet to high heat. Add 2 T oil to the pan. Once the pan is hot, pour half the batter (about two cups) into the pan, using a silicone spatula to help spread it out evenly and quickly. After a minute or so, shake the pan to make sure the pancake doesn't stick.

6. Continue cooking on high heat until bubbles break and remain open on top of the pancake and the edges begin to look dry. Using a spatula, carefully lift one side of the pancake to make sure the pancake is speckled dark brown in places.

7. Now you're ready to flip! Carefully slide the pancake out of the pan and onto one of the plates. Quickly cover with the other plate and flip. Then, with the help of the spatula if necessary, slide the pancake back into the pan, uncooked side down.

8. Press the pancake into the pan and shake to make sure it doesn't stick. Reduce the heat to medium. Continue cooking until the bottom is brown and the pancake is cooked through, about 3–5 minutes more.

9. Slide the cooked pancake onto a heatproof cutting board. Cover with aluminum foil while you repeat with the other half of the batter.

10. Using a serrated knife or a pizza cutter, cut each pancake into 8 wedges.

11. Serve with spicy soy dipping sauce.

Spicy Soy Dipping Sauce

———

This is my no-muss, no-fuss, go-to Korean flavor bomb. Honestly, you can put it together with pantry ingredients in under five minutes. It pairs with the Red Moon Mandu and Veggie Pajeon recipes in this chapter. But I also use it as a marinade for chicken and pork. You can also toss veggies in it before roasting.

Ingredients:

4 T tamari soy sauce
3 T rice wine vinegar
1 T rice syrup or agave nectar
1 T gojuchang
1 t sesame oil
1 T white sesame seeds, toasted
1 T black sesame seeds, toasted (if unavailable, just use 2 T white sesame seeds)

1. Add soy sauce, vinegar, sweetener, gojuchang, and sesame oil in a medium bowl. Whisk thoroughly to completely incorporate the gojuchang.
2. Divide the mixture between four small bowls for dipping. Top each bowl with 1/4 t white and 1/4 t black sesame seeds.

Roasted Veggie Japchae Salad

———

Potluck suppers in college towns are the crossroads of the world. Crunchy taquitos next to soothing saag paneer; Hearty baked ziti crowded beside a lacy fougasse. Universities attract people from around the world as faculty, administrators, and students. And happily, they often see get-togethers as an opportunity to share a part of their culture.

Another thing about college towns is that people come and go. Students come for a time and move on. Faculty members leave for sabbaticals. Researchers leave to collect data. It's just the natural order of things, but sometimes, those departures leave a hole—especially on the buffet table.

This happened a few years ago when Hyang-Sook, one of my college's graduate students, was ready to take her first faculty position, leaving us without one of my favorite buffet staples: japchae, tender sweet potato noodles, slippery with soy sauce, topped with spinach and other veggies. Although the dish is traditionally a noodle dish topped with thinly sliced beef, Hyang-Sook's version was vegan to accommodate the college's many vegetarians, and it was served at room temperature. I was so sad at the thought of never eating it again that I asked her for her recipe. And she kindly sent me a link to Beyond Kimchee (beyondkimchee.com), a fantastic website run by Korean food writer Hyegyoung "Holly" Ford, the author of *Korean Cooking Favorites*.

I love Holly's original recipe, and I've made it many times, but I also realized I could enjoy those tangy noodles more often if I could find a way to fit them into my typical weeknight routine. The sweet potato starch noodles were easy—they're available dry in any Asian or Korean market. To make the rest of the meal a bit easier, I decided to focus on vegetables I almost always have in the house: peppers, Brussels sprouts, mushrooms, and green beans. Then I tossed them all with a gingery rice wine vinaigrette and roasted them in a hot oven while I was making the rest of the salad. (In summer, you can grill the veggies over a charcoal grill.) Spinach is a traditional japchae component, but one that required another cooking technique—*not* weeknight-friendly. So instead, I added some finely shredded cabbage to the salad, which added a nice bit of freshness and crunch. If I have a cooked chicken breast around, I'll toss it on top of the noodles along with the veggies. But honestly, I love it just as well without it. The final result is a potluck wonder: great at room temperature, happy to sit on the buffet table while you discuss the book, and an awesome leftover. Although, there's rarely any leftover.

Equipment you will need: a colander, kitchen shears

Equipment that would be nice: a Microplane grater; a garlic press

Ingredients:

For the roasted vegetables:
8 oz Brussels sprouts
1 red onion
1 red bell pepper
1 yellow bell pepper
8 oz mushrooms (shiitakes are traditional, but I use whatever's on hand)
4 oz green beans (preferable thin, such as haricots verts)
4 T neutral oil, such as canola or grapeseed
3 T rice wine vinegar
2 T soy sauce
1 T doenjang
2-inch piece of ginger
2 cloves garlic

To complete the salad:
8 oz sweet potato noodles (sometimes labeled glass noodles or dangmyeon)
3 T neutral oil
2 T soy sauce
1 T fish sauce
2 T rice wine vinegar
1 t sesame oil
1 T white sesame seeds
1 T black sesame seeds (or just use 2 T white sesame seeds)

1. Heat the oven to 400 degrees Fahrenheit.
2. Trim any damaged leaves off the Brussels sprouts. Cut them in half and core them, removing the hard portion by cutting a small triangle out of each. Place in a large mixing bowl.
3. Peel the onion. Cut in half through the stem end. Lay both halves flat and cut into 1/2-inch slices, from top to bottom. Add to the Brussels sprouts in the mixing bowl.
4. Core and seed the bell peppers. Cut into 1/2-inch slices, from top to bottom. Add to the veggies in the bowl.
5. Remove the stems from the mushrooms and discard (or save for mushroom broth). Slice the caps into 1/2-inch slices. Add to the veggies in the bowl.
6. Trim the green bean ends. Add to the veggies in the bowl.
7. Combine the oil, vinegar, soy sauce, and doenjang in a small bowl. Using a Microplane grater, grate the ginger into the bowl. Alternatively, you can mince the ginger finely with a chef's knife and add it to the bowl. Press the garlic into the bowl or mince it with a chef's knife and add it to the bowl. Stir to combine the vinaigrette ingredients thoroughly.
8. Add the ginger vinaigrette to the vegetables in the bowl and toss to make sure the vegetables are evenly coated. Place the vegetables onto a rimmed baking sheet big enough to hold them in a single layer, if you have one. Roast in middle of the oven for about 15 minutes.
9. Using a spatula, toss the veggies about halfway through to make sure they're browned evenly on both sides. (It's fine if you need to divide them between two baking sheets— just rotate them bottom to top and front to back when you're tossing them halfway through the cooking time.) Return to the oven for 10–15 minutes, until the vegetables

are soft and browned in places. Remove from the oven and allow to cool on the pan.

10. Meanwhile, cook the sweet potato noodles according to the package directions. They should be soft and slippery with a bit of chew, but not at all hard. Drain the noodles in a colander and run under cold water to stop the cooking. Then—here's the fun part—take the kitchen shears in one hand and a handful of noodles in the other and cut the noodles into more manageable portions. Repeat until all the noodles are cut. Add the noodles to a salad bowl or large pasta serving bowl.

11. Combine the oil, soy sauce, fish sauce, vinegar, and sesame oil in a small bowl. Whisk together and pour over the noodles, gentle tossing until all the noodles strands are covered.

12. When the vegetables are cooled, artfully place them on top of the dressed noodles. If not serving immediately, cover the salad with plastic wrap and refrigerate. The salad can sit in the refrigerator for a couple of hours— bring it to room temperature before serving.

13. Garnish with white and black sesame seeds just before serving.

Fruit (& Egg) Salad Inspired by Chun Hyang's Love Song

If you start cooking Korean food on your own, you are sure to come across one of the YouTube videos of Korean food authority Maangchi at some point. Author of *Maangchi's Big Book of Korean Food*, she is as much-loved by her fans for her whimsical personality as she is for her fantastic food. Her recipes really work, so she can get me to try just about anything. When the love song from Chun Hyang, which has a few stanzas where the lovers discuss tempting fruits for dinner, inspired me to create a fruit salad for this book, I naturally turned to Maangchi for a traditional Korean starting point. Here, I was met with a rare cultural divide I had some trouble crossing.

The first surprise came in the form of some ingredients Americans aren't used to seeing in a fruit salad. Cucumbers, for example, although their freshness and crispiness made me wonder why I'd never included them before. The hard-boiled egg, however, was more of a shock. It seemed so out of place. But this led to the second surprise: the salad Maangchi described was truly a side dish, not the "virtuous dessert choice" that many Americans would expect. It was firmly on the savory side. And that was because of the third surprise, which proved the most difficult stumbling block: the dressing was a simple combination of mayo and yellow mustard. I made the recipe as written and was surprised again because it was really interesting, in a savory kind of way. But it definitely didn't fill the place on the buffet table where my US book clubbers needed to put a fruit salad.

I had to remind myself that sometimes those cultural gaps will happen—and it's okay. I have stretched my basic Irish-American-girl palate a long way, and there are some places it's just not willing to go. (I'm looking at you, haggis.) And almost everyone I know has some food they simply can't get past. You can look everywhere in this book, and you won't find a single beet—because I think they taste like dirt.

Not willing to give up on the idea of a fruit salad, I decided what I needed was some fusion. First, I looked at the tasty items mentioned in the love song: watermelon, cucumber (there it was again), eggplant (no help there), honey, apples, grapes, cherries, and apricots. It was actually a pretty good start to a fruit salad. Next, I looked at some of the elements that made the Korean versions so distinct from what we're used to in the US. After asking for a lot of opinions, it looked like the eggs were a non-starter for most of my friends and family—even the adventurous eaters didn't seem to like the idea.

One element that I loved in Maangchi's recipe was salty peanuts. Salty-sweet is my happy place, so I knew I wanted to incorporate them into my own recipe. Another idea I loved was putting dried fruit in the salad. Her recipe also had dried cranberries. I'm not the biggest fan, but looking at the ingredients from the song, I realized dried apricots would solve the problem of trying to include a fruit that seems to be perfect for exactly one week each summer!

When it came to the dressing, I thought immediately of a recipe a Dutch camp counselor gave me that included yogurt and cinnamon. Always looking for non-dairy options for potlucks, I decided to swap in unsweetened coconut milk yogurt. The cinnamon was already on-point for Korean cuisine. I grabbed the honey from the love song, and a dressing was born.

Ingredients:

16 oz watermelon spears*
16 oz cantaloupe, honeydew, or other sweet melon spears (or a combination)*
1 English cucumber
20 white seedless grapes
2 gala apples
1 Asian pear
1 c canned sweet cherries, well-drained
1 c unsweetened coconut milk Greek yogurt
2 T – 1/4 c honey, depending on how sweet you like your fruit salad (I use the lower amount)
1/4 t ground cinnamon, plus a bit more to garnish
1/2 c dry roasted peanuts, salted or lightly salted

3 or 4 mint leaves (optional)

2 hard-boiled eggs (completely optional)

1. Cut the melon spears into 1-inch pieces. Add to a large bowl.
2. Peel the cucumber. Slice it in half the long way. Using the tip of a spoon, scoop out the seeds. Cut each half the long way again and cut the spears into 1-inch pieces. Add to the bowl.
3. Slice the grapes in half through the stem end. Add to the bowl.
4. Peel the apples. Cut in four pieces through the core. Remove the core and cut the apples into 1-inch pieces. Add to the bowl.
5. Peel the Asian pear. Cut in four pieces through the core. Remove the core and cut the pear into 1-inch pieces.
6. Using a colander, drain the cherries, shaking gently to remove as much of the canning liquid as possible. Add the drained cherries to the bowl.
7. In a small bowl, mix the yogurt, honey, and cinnamon together until completely smooth. Using a rubber spatula, scrape the yogurt mixture into the fruit bowl. Toss the peanuts on top of the salad. If you're using the eggs, cut them in half lengthwise, and then again, lengthwise.
8. Using the spatula, gently fold the dressing into the fruit until all of the fruit is uniformly coated. Dust the top with a bit more cinnamon, if desired.
9. Stack the mint leaves on top of one another. Roll like a cigar from the stem end. Thinly slice the mint "cigar" to chiffonade. Separate the strands of mint and arrange on top of the salad.

*Note: While I usually hate the idea of paying the premium to have someone else prepare my fruits and veggies, this salad is one time I take advantage of the help. My local grocery store almost always has a 32 oz Triple Melon combo consisting of watermelon, cantaloupe, and honeydew spears. I love the convenience of it, along with not needing to store and find a way to use the leftover melon. But you can certainly buy the whole fruit, use what you need, and store the rest.

Take Book Club to the Next Level: The Tale of Chun Hyang

———

BEVERAGES TO OFFER:

Non-alcoholic drinks: Chun Hyang and Li Mong share tea when he comes to her mother's house. But that doesn't necessarily mean a drink made from traditional tea leaves. *Bori-cha*, or barley tea, is a very traditional Korean infusion of roasted barley soaked in boiling water. According to Sue Pressey, creator of the *My Korean Kitchen* website and author of The Banchan Cookbook, barley tea is offered instead of water in many Korean homes, and it's one of the first food items offered to Korean babies (cooled down, of course). The pre-roasted grain is widely available in Asian markets—all you have to do is simmer it for about five minutes. But if you can't find it, you can simply roast pearl barley in a 375-degree oven until it's deeply browned and smells toasty. Another popular infusion is *sujeonggwa*, a lightly sweetened cinnamon and ginger tea that reminds me of mulled wine. It can be served either warm or iced, garnished with pine nuts. It's easy enough to make yourself with cinnamon sticks, fresh ginger, and brown sugar. Even easier—Asian markets carry cinnamon-ginger tea bags!

Alcoholic drinks: Wine is mentioned more than thirty times in my translation of *The Tale of Chun Hyang*! Rice wine has been central to Korean cuisine for thousands of years, but there are many iterations. According to Caroline Hatchett, writing for Liquor.com, the rice fermentation process begins with rice, water, and *nuruk*, a kind of Korean "sourdough starter" in the form of a grain cake that dries and molds in a lengthy, controlled process. The first step in the fermentation process is *wonju*, a cloudy, high-alcohol liquor. It is normally allowed to settle, and the clear *chungju* is skimmed off the top—this beverage is a lot like Japan's better-known sake.

MUSIC TO PLAY/VIDEOS TO STREAM:

Pansori music, of course! Spotify users can access a twenty-hour playlist called Pansori: Korean Classical Music. Even better, during the COVID-19 pandemic, the National Gugak Theatre in Korea shared content for audiences who couldn't leave their homes. On day three of the series, they shared "Sarangga," the famous love song from *The Tale of Chunhyang*. That performance is available on YouTube at https://www.youtube.com/watch?v=bSTms9qkcI4. A number of movie versions of the pansori exist—some are available on streaming services, but the infamous North Korean version is available for free. Even if you don't want to waste precious book club time watching videos, understanding the original nature of the Korean operatic performance, and seeing how it has been interpreted most recently can add another dimension to your understanding of the tale. Those looking for a follow-up might enjoy streaming the 2020 Korean film *The Pansori Singer*, a historical romance that tells the story of an itinerant entertainer traveling through Korea looking for his kidnapped wife. The movie received a number of award nominations at festivals and includes historical representations of pansori performances.

WHAT TO BRING/TABLESCAPES:

No Korean meal is complete without rice and soup. If you have a rice cooker or Instant Pot, making a pot of perfect rice is simple. But it's just as easy to buy a few containers from a local Korean restaurant. Likewise, the simplest Korean soup can be made by heating doenjang and broth, then garnishing with tofu and green onions. You can certainly do it on your own, but it's easy enough to pick up soup from a Korean grocer or restaurant. Include a range of different kimchis and other condiments for book club members to try—asking for help in an Asian grocery can yield all kinds of delicious banchan and mitbanchan—ask which ones are traditional. To set the table properly, you'll need chopsticks and a soup spoon, along with a range of dishes for condiments, including soy sauce and gojuchang.

On Eating like a Local in Seoul

———

I'll admit that when I went to Seoul, Korea, as a graduate student in 2002, I was pretty much jet-lagged the whole time. I was presenting a paper at my first international conference, leaving my husband and daughters behind on my first trip to Asia. I was both absolutely terrified and absolutely thrilled. I flew from Gainesville to Atlanta, then had a twelve-hour, non-stop flight to Seoul. I arrived exhausted, and I never really had a chance to catch up on sleep. I didn't have the luxury of going a day or two early and beating the jetlag because money was tight (as I said, I was a graduate student), and my husband was juggling a full-time job, a precocious third grader, and a toddler all at once to make the adventure possible. So, it was a "go in, deliver the paper, see the sights if you can, get out" operation.

It sounds terrible, but it wasn't at all. In fact, it wound up being one of the highlights of my graduate career. Because in spite of the sleep deprivation, I was able to share the time with some amazing friends. My alma mater, the University of Florida, is home to a proud contingent of "Korean Gators." And when they found out my Bulgarian friend Daniela and I were going to be on their home turf, they made it their business to ensure we had the best possible experience. I know we went to Gyeongbokgung Palace (in a torrential downpour, with Eyun-Ki daintily stepping over cobblestones in open-toed sandals) and Seoul Tower (beautiful view, I'm told, if it isn't cloudy). But what I remember most about that trip are the meals. Even now, just walking into a Korean restaurant brings me back to that sticky, exciting week.

Walking into a Korean restaurant with friends was so much different than my morning forays into the surrounding neighborhood to save money by avoiding the hotel breakfast. In the mornings, I was cautious, self-conscious, and stressed: I found a tiny shop near the hotel that served soup and banchan and just had that and a cup of barley tea every morning. If there was anything else on the menu, I never found out—I just ate what the lady brought me.

But each of the evenings we were there, a different group of Gators made sure we had a local escort to dinner. And that was the most fun thing ever. One of my favorite memories was the night when Moon arranged for us to eat at a traditional Korean BBQ restaurant. The smell of caramelized meat and funky kimchi almost knocked me over when I walked through the door. Moon acted as hostess and taught us the etiquette of eating out in Seoul. Never pour your own drink. Never stand your chopsticks upright into a bowl of rice. Wait until the senior person at the table eats.

Sometimes the food was so spicy that Daniela and I mostly ate rice, at least one night. I tried to hang with the locals and wound up putting out the fire with way more soju than was probably a good idea. After beer and more food and more soju and more food, we finally left the restaurant. We walked around the student area, Myeong-dong, and watched the students play games in the video bang. I remember feeling like even though I didn't have a lot of time in Seoul, I got to know it because I had eaten so many meals with locals. Not only that, those people are still special to me. I don't see them all the time or speak with them frequently. But they're friends I seek out when we're at conferences. I always try to plan a meal with them, if I can.

A REGENCY ROMANCE RE-READ

Photo credit: Lee Ahern

The Book Recommendation: Pride and Prejudice

———

How long has it been since you read *Pride and Prejudice*? Do you know it as well as you think you do?

Did you skim it during a semester of comparative literature, between reading *Middlemarch* and *Tess of the d'Urbervilles*? Did you take a copy on a beach vacation and lose yourself in the characters? You've probably watched the movies—the real one with Colin Firth or the fake one with Keira Knightley—along with a pint of Chunky Monkey after a bad breakup. You probably recognize the first line, and maybe you've even riffed on it yourself: "It is a truth universally acknowledged that a single man in possession of a surfboard is in search of a wave."

But what if you hadn't? What if you could open it up like any other novel on your "To Be Read" pile without knowing what was about to happen? Do you think you'd still be taken in by Wickham? Would you see yourself in Jane or Lizzy? Would you feel more sympathy for the annoying members of the older generation trying to manage the world in favor of their children? Would you still think Lizzy made the right choice in the end?

Maybe you feel like you know *Pride and Prejudice* so well, you don't need to go back—or you wouldn't want to. But I'm asking you to rethink it. You're not the same person you were when you read P&P the first time—so why would you expect it to be the same book? And if you haven't read *Pride and Prejudice* with a group of friends, really dug into the characters, and tried to understand why they do the things they do, I don't think you've had the complete experience.

Modern-day readers tend to think of *Pride and Prejudice* as the prototypical English-language romance novel. That's not unfair, considering that the romance novel industry was born from what we'd now call "fan fiction," when Georgette Heyer started writing novels set in the Regency period to fill the void that Jane Austen's early death had created. But *Pride and Prejudice* is so much more than a romance!

What if it's actually a book about women and culture and power? What if we chose to reread a novel we all think we know, in a manner that shifts our focus away from the various love stories and directs it toward the complex relationships that women engage in throughout the novel? For example, if we set aside the concept of female rivalry in securing a husband, we can focus better on how Lizzy's friendship with Charlotte is tested throughout the novel by each young woman's developing perspectives on the role of marriage. By doing that, we would gain critical insights into the culture that Austen herself was trying to represent. In fact, rereading *Pride and Prejudice* with your book club could be like an archaeological dig, each chapter revealing tidbits about the day-to-day life of women in England during the early nineteenth century.

The novel opens with a slice of marital life, as Mrs. Bennet is imploring her husband to introduce himself to Mr. Bingley, a new single resident of the area, so that he may, in turn, introduce him to his five eligible daughters. But it also introduces a complex web of interpersonal relationships that impact the Bennet's lives throughout the book. Lady Lucas, for example, must be cultivated so that she can use her higher social status to provide introductions to eligible suitors for the Bennet sisters. But she is also a rival, as eligible bachelors are a limited resource, and she has her own family to marry off. The interplay between the matrons with marriageable daughters throughout the novel is the definition of the word "frenemies."

The bonds among the Bennet sisters form another interesting focus for a reread. Lizzy, as the central figure in the book, is fiercely protective of all her sisters, although she sees their faults quite clearly. Perhaps this makes sense in a society where the actions of one member of the family affected all members of the family. But it's Lizzy's relationship with Jane, the oldest and most beautiful of the Bennet sisters, that centers the narrative. Lizzy is the first to support her sister's budding romance with Bingley, and the main action of the novel derives from Lizzy's fierce reaction to Mr.

Darcy's misplaced distrust of her. Similarly, Lizzy's strong reaction to the implications of Lydia's behavior on the rest of her family unwittingly hands Darcy the tools to mend their relationship. Considering the significance of Darcy's sister Georgiana, Mrs. Bennet's sister Mrs. Phillips, and the conniving Bingley sisters, it might not be a stretch to say that *Pride and Prejudice* is actually a story about the power of sibling relationships.

I love recommending a reread for book clubs because it allows the members to compare their current selves and past selves. And in most book clubs, all those past selves weren't friends yet, so it's like introducing people to a previous version of you. I suggest you take an ethnographic approach to the text and try to learn from it, as you would a piece of non-fiction. Taking the "student" point of view allows you to discover new things in familiar territory, which is the goal of a reread. I've read dozens of *P&P* retellings, and all of them had something to offer, but sometimes only the OG will do.

The World of Elizabeth and Darcy

So, what was going on in Elizabeth and Darcy's world? Let's start with America's favorite villain-king, George III, whose madness gave us what we now know as The Regency in 1810. Years of his wars around the globe, including the American Revolution, the Peninsular Wars, and the War of 1812, left the Crown *very* short of cash. The wars also cost the country the lives of many young men who might otherwise have been working as tenant farmers on wealthy estates. A culinary impact of the wars: they impacted the flow of wine and brandy from France to England.

Outside of Europe, the monopolistic British East India Company continued to consolidate its power in India, which eventually led to the British Raj in 1858, fueling the ever-increasing wealth of the merchant class. It's important to remember that Mr. Darcy and Mr. Bingley are just that: Misters. When we first hear of Mr. Bingley, remember, he is described as being from the "North," which is the industrial heartland of England. It's also mentioned that the Bingley sisters tend to "forget" that their brother's wealth is from trade. Bingley and Darcy's importance hint at the reduced power of the aristocracy and gentry, whose wealth was based on land. The increasing wealth of the upper classes leads to their increased patronage of the arts and architecture, allowing the wealthy to physically manifest their newfound money in extravagant estates, such as Pemberley.

The expansion of the British Empire also increased the availability of all kinds of tropical goods, many of which found their way onto tables across England. The highly stratified nature of English society meant that the wealthy few were able to employ lots of help for every possible task in their opulent households. Men and women worked in a wide range of unskilled and skilled positions, from kitchen maids and stable hands to butlers and housekeepers. The surfeit of household labor had implications for fashion—hairstyles and clothing that required help to be worn properly—as well as cuisine, with meals of many different dishes and courses routinely eaten by the upper classes.

The expanding free time of women of the upper classes also had ramifications for their education. In addition to reading, writing, and basic math, women were increasingly given education in the arts, with expectations for accomplishment in painting, music, dancing, and singing—all documented in Austen's works.

Young women of the upper classes led lives constrained by society's emphasis on their purity. They were constantly chaperoned, their bodies and behaviors subject to constant public scrutiny. There are a very limited set of circumstances under which men and women were able to interact without violating social mores. These included balls, dinners, open carriage rides, and walks in public areas. But a smart woman might make the system work in her favor. Austen illustrates this when Mrs. Bennet, anticipating rain, leaves Jane without a carriage after a visit, so the Bingleys are compelled to ask her to stay.

But the expectation of and appreciation for women's private accomplishments did not carry over into the public sphere. Gender lines continued to be clearly drawn, and most women could not legally own or inherit property in England, which is one of the crisis points in *Pride and Prejudice*. Married women derived their social standing from their husband's, while spinsters were reliant on male members of their families—fathers, brothers, uncles, cousins, and brothers-in-law—for support and legal protection.

Intentionally or not, Jane Austen does an outstanding job relating the frustration and insecurity women faced in such a social system. Without avenues toward independence, women's well-being depended on creating and maintaining a complex web of relationships. Acquiring a husband was the first and most obvious step for a young woman in securing her future, which is no doubt why marriages are such significant plot points in the novel, and even the imperfect pairings, such as Charlotte Lucas with Mr. Collins, which puts her in line to be mistress of Longbourne, are greeted with general relief:

The whole family, in short, were properly overjoyed on the occasion. The younger girls formed hopes of coming out a year or two sooner than they might otherwise have done; and the boys were relieved from their apprehension of Charlotte's dying an old maid. Charlotte herself was tolerably composed. She had gained her point, and had time to consider it. Her reflections were in general satisfactory. Mr. Collins, to be sure, was neither sensible nor agreeable; his society was irksome, and his attachment to her must be imaginary. But still he would be her husband. Without thinking highly either of men or matrimony, marriage had always been her object; it was the only provision for well-educated young women of small fortune, and however uncertain of giving happiness, must be their pleasantest preservative from want.

The sly humor that permeates *Pride and Prejudice*, as the foibles of the main characters are subsequently exposed, is likely one of the reasons for the lasting popularity of the novel. Jane Austen undertakes a self-deprecating and candid examination of her social world and is not afraid to find it wanting. And the reader feels like they're in on the joke. What are your favorite examples of humor in P&P, and what point is Austen trying to make about her world with it? Sounds like a great way to kick off discussion at book club.

Essentials of Regency English Cuisine

———

There are plenty of contemporary sources describing food in the Regency era, but one of the most interesting is the house book of Martha Lloyd, a friend who lived with the members of the Austen family for many years. House books were collections of accounts and other information pertinent to running a house. House books often included recipes to ensure that favorite dishes could be duplicated, and Martha Lloyd's had many of them reflecting the epicurean trends of the time. Not surprisingly, many of those dishes found their way into the novels Jane Austen was writing at the time, according to Julienne Gehrer, the editor responsible for *Martha Lloyd's Household Book*, which reproduces her house book, page for page and food stain by food stain, to share with contemporary audiences interested in all things Jane Austen.

House books—and indeed, most pre-twentieth century recipes—were not written with great precision. Most often, they listed a collection of ingredients and very general instructions, assuming the reader knew the general steps necessary to turn leeks, broth, wine, and potatoes into a hearty soup. To help out modern audiences who were familiar with systematic measurement and step-by-step directions, historical cookbook author Maggie Black translated and codified some of Lloyd's original recipes in *The Jane Austen Cookbook.*

Of course, one set of recipes from a household of limited means and its own tastes and predilections can't describe the whole cuisine of Regency England. In particular, it does not describe the kinds of extravagant dishes encountered by the wealthiest members of society, such as the Bingleys and the Darcys. While researching the Nerd Night talk on food and books that eventually led to this book, I looked at a wide range of early published cookbooks and some scholarly work on British food history and found five types of ingredients that seem to define Regency English cuisine: dairy products, meat and offal; imported spices; fortified wines; and fresh citrus fruit.

DAIRY PRODUCTS

Going through vintage British cookbooks, one thing that stands out for the modern cookbook lover is the lack of oil—not an olive or canola in sight. So, there is little chance that Elizabeth and Darcy were staying healthy with a Mediterranean diet. That's because dairy was ubiquitous, a feature of the country's system of tenant farming. But without refrigeration, milk quickly became a breeding ground for bacteria—not what one contemporary food authority would describe as "good eats." Butter- and cheese-making were the answer to making the abundant cow and sheep milk shelf-stable, and

Regency recipes make extensive use of both. Butter shows up in every course, from whets (that's appetizers) to pudding (dessert, which isn't necessarily always pudding). So, we know that dinner would have been rich, with lots of caramelized meats and veggies, silky sauces, and delectable desserts. The Foods of England Project, the authority on historical British cuisine, lists recipes (or "receipts" as they call them) for a fanciful range of dairy desserts, including junket, curd loaf, posset, and multitudinous syllabubs, a whipped cream dessert fortified with alcohol.

MEAT AND OFFAL

At least among the wealthy, meat ruled the Regency table. But dinner wasn't just about prime cuts. Today's nose-to-tail chefs take inspiration from former generations' use of offal. A whole, boiled calf's head was often the centerpiece for a dinner party. The Foods of England Project lists a recipe of one stuffed with a brain-and-bread pudding and, of course, served with clarified butter. Regency cooks were expected to wring all the nutrition possible out of every animal. Cowheel Bones were made into broth. Suet (beef fat) and lard (pig fat) were rendered, adding more shelf-stable fats to the Regency pantry. And while beef was king, lamb and pork were also abundant.

Hunting was still common during the time period, and game made up a substantial part of the Regency diet. Cookbooks included recipes like "Kentish Plover" and "Sparrow Dumplings." But the most interesting thing for me was the way meat found its way into the dessert course. Most contemporary Americans only see that on Thanksgiving, when Aunt

Loretta serves up a traditional mincemeat pie. But Regency eaters would not have been surprised to complete their meal with Calf's Foot Jelly, a kind of sweet aspic. Or Marrow Tarts, which were a custard pie featuring bone marrow. Or Spotted Dog, a steamed suet pudding made with dried fruits and served with crème anglaise, rather like a traditional Christmas pudding.

IMPORTED SPICES

Spices were an important part of the pantries of the upper classes in England from the Middle Ages. But it wasn't until much later that they filtered down to the general public. The first trip of what eventually became the British East India Company came back to England with Indonesian peppercorns. However, the British got tired of fighting with the colonialist Dutch in Indonesia and finally focused their own colonial energies on India, where they slowly consolidated power over the course of two hundred years. Fun fact: the treaty that finally gave the Moluccan island Run, a center of nutmeg production, over to the Dutch, ceded a little island called Manhattan to the English in return—and it's only fair to note that the Dutch were generally seen to have gotten the best of the bargain by contemporary commentators. Spices were the backbone of the British East India Company's operation. Chief among the imports were cloves, mace, nutmeg, and cinnamon, and these increasingly found their way onto Regency tables.

One unintended consequence of civil servants and soldiers living in India for long and formative periods of their lives was that it raised their expectations about food actually tasting interesting when they got back to England. The first curry shop in London—the brainchild of Sake Dean Mahomet—opened in 1810, forever improving lunchtime in the British capital. But it's important to remember that early British curries represent something of a cultural fusion. Hannah Glasse's 1747 *Art of Cookery, Made Plain and Easy* included a recipe to "make currey the Indian way" that listed Britain's ubiquitous butter and a pint of cream, along with the traditional turmeric, ginger, and pepper.

FORTIFIED WINES

England's cold and rainy climate wasn't exactly hospitable to creating its own viniculture. But that didn't mean they couldn't appreciate wine—and even attempt to make their own. Historical British cookbooks include recipes for wine made from turnips, treacle, and even cowslip. But the English aristocracy, who were largely descended from the French warriors that sailed over with William the Conqueror in 1066, remained appreciative of French wines. According to Joshua Malin writing for vinepair.com, when Eleanor of Aquitaine brought Bordeaux under English sovereignty through her marriage to Henry II, the English finally had a cheap, reliable source of French wine. In fact, the British drank so much red wine that their preferences came to shape what the vineyards produced, giving the world "claret."

Once the English crown no longer controlled parts of France, the wine trade was interrupted periodically by wars between France and England. Looking beyond France for their wine fix, the English merchants ventured to other historical wine regions, such as Spain and Portugal. But the sea voyage necessary to import those wines could be long and rough—a real problem for the thin, glass bottles. To make the trade profitable, fortification of wine was necessary. Adding spirits to the wine stopped the fermentation process and made it more stable for sea voyages. So sweet, heavily fortified wines became a staple of Regency cuisine. The stronger, sweeter wine appealed to English tastes—in fact, during the Regency era, men routinely left the dining table to enjoy a digestif of port, while the ladies withdrew for tea. And once fortified wines were in the house, it wasn't long before they wound up in the kitchen. *The Foods of England Project* contains recipes for duck, beef heart, and kidneys served with fortified wine sauces. Cakes and puddings swam in Madiera and sherry, including that staple of the holiday table, Christmas Pudding.

FRESH CITRUS FRUIT

Like grapes, citrus is outside the British grow-zone. Trade relationships with Spain and Portugal provided some citrus imports, but by the nineteenth century, a great deal was grown in and exported from the British colonies in India and the Caribbean. The high cost of importation meant citrus (aside from the dried peel) was a prestige item in Regency England. Wanting to assure themselves of a supply of oranges and lemons, the wealthy began including orangeries—conservatories optimized for growing tropical and sub-tropical fruit trees—into their increasingly fantastic home designs. Citrus found its way into all kinds of foods, from beverages and sauces to desserts. And for those not wealthy enough to have access to fresh citrus, the flavor could still be found in recipes like Orange Peel Pie (which was, in actuality, an apple pie scented with reconstituted orange peel).

PRIDE AND PREJUDICE: RECIPES FOR BOOK CLUB

"You must and shall be married by a special license. But my dearest love, tell me what dish Mr. Darcy is particularly fond of, that I may have it tomorrow."

Zucchini Soup
with Stilton

———

This recipe combines three items absolutely essential to the Regency English table: fresh vegetables and herbs from the kitchen garden; luscious, full-fat dairy products; and a hint of fruity Spanish sherry. I admit to having a brown thumb myself, but I'm lucky enough to live in a community where local farmers' market tables groan under the weight of local produce all summer long. This is a soup you can enjoy in August and September when zucchini come five for a dollar. And it's even better when those green-thumbed friends of yours drop zucchinis off at your doorstep, happy you'll turn it into something wonderful.

Stilton is a very assertive blue cheese that's been made in rural England since at least the early eighteenth century. In fact, the little town of Melton Mowbray, Leicestershire, where it was first cataloged, is not far from Hertfordshire, the place many scholars believe Austen set her fictional Longbourne. I love it in small amounts to add a bit of funk and a lot of umami to vegetable-forward dishes. If it's hard to get where you are, you can get fantastic results with other strong blue cheeses, like Roquefort from France, Cabrales from Spain, or even Iowa's own Maytag Blue. And if you're making it for people who aren't accustomed to blue cheese at all, you could use a very mild version, such as Danablue, a super mild blue cheese from Denmark.

Yield: 4 medium or 8 small servings

Equipment you will need: either a stick blender, blender, or food processor for pureeing the soup

Ingredients:

1 ¾–2 lb zucchini (about 3 large or 5 small)
3 ½ T unsalted butter (divided)
1 large yellow onion, chopped
2 t kosher salt (divided)
½ t dried mustard powder
2 c chicken or veggie broth
½ c water
3 springs fresh thyme, leaves removed (or 1 t dried)
1 sprig fresh rosemary, leaves removed and chopped (or 2 t dried)
1 c half and half
1 T sherry
1 T fresh lemon juice
4 oz Stilton cheese, crumbled (divided)
Salt and ground white pepper

1. Rinse the zucchini and rub the skins vigorously under running water to remove any grit. Trim the bottoms and tops from the zucchini. Cut in half the long way, then cut in half the long way again. Cut the zucchini quarters into 1-inch, quarter-moon slices. Place the zucchini in a medium bowl and set aside.

2. Place a Dutch oven or sturdy pot over medium heat. When the pot is hot, add 2 ½ T butter.

3. When the butter has melted, add the zucchini and 1 t salt to the pot. Coat the zucchini pieces with the butter and turn up the heat slightly. Sauté the zucchini, stirring frequently, so that all the pieces start to get brown in spots and become soft. Remove the zucchini from the pot.

4. Over medium heat, add the remaining 1 T butter to the pot. When the butter has melted, add the onions and 1 t salt. Sauté the onions until they are softened and turning golden, about 5–7 minutes. Add the dried mustard and sauté for 1 minute more.

5. Return the zucchini to the pot. Add the broth and water to the pot and bring to a boil. Reduce heat to a simmer and cook for 30 minutes, half-covering the pot to reduce evaporation, adding broth or water if necessary to assure the zucchini are still floating and do not dry out and stick to the bottom of the pan. Remove from heat. The zucchini should be quite soft. Add the herbs to the zucchini mixture, either in the pot if you are using a stick blender, or in the blender or food processor if that's what you're using.

6. Puree the soup in a blender or food processor (in batches if necessary), wipe out the pot, and return to the pan. Alternatively, use a stick blender to puree the soup in the pot.

7. Over medium heat, return the soup to a simmer. Add the half and half and sherry. Mix thoroughly and gently bring to a simmer without boiling. Add the lemon juice, combining thoroughly. At this point, test the consistency of the soup. If it's too thick for you, add a little water or extra broth; bring back to a strong simmer. Stir in half the Stilton. Season with salt and white pepper to taste.
8. Divide the soup between four bowls. Divide the remaining Stilton between the four bowls for garnish.
9. To serve a larger group, the soup can be served in shot glasses, as part of a buffet table.

Vegan Blueberry Scones

———

It was a breakdown on the D train that led to my love of scones. Sometime in the early 1990s, when I was the managing editor of a trade magazine called *Marine Log*, I worked with a freelance writer whose other gig was at a magazine called *Colonial Homes*. Bob always brought by the latest issue of *CH* when it was out, which was both sweet and completely unnecessary, as at the time I was a single, twenty-something living in a brownstone in Park Slope, Brooklyn, and the farthest thing from my mind was decorating a house, colonial or otherwise. But since I had a forty-five-minute subway commute from the city every day, I often stuffed the issue into my tote—in case I ran out of reading material.

I was lucky enough to have a seat when my train stopped. After about five minutes, the conductor came over the scratchy PA system and told us we were going to be there a while. I rifled through my tote for something to pass the time and found an issue of *Colonial Homes*. Passing quickly through the design tips and antique insights, I came to an article titled "Scones!" by Joanne L. Hayes. In it, she shared recipes for more than a dozen types of scones, from traditional English tea scones to a heart-shaped scone filled with cherry jam perfect for Valentine's Day. Maybe it was just because I was looking at a much-delayed dinner, but they sounded amazing. I went home, turned on the oven, and despite the fact that I'd rarely baked anything that didn't start with a Betty Crocker box in my life, baked my first batch of scones: orange-sesame. They were fantastic, nutty from the sesame seeds, fragrant with orange rind, and I've made that recipe, as well as some of the others in *Colonial Homes* article, many times since then. In fact, I still have the yellowed pages I tore out of the magazine all those years ago.

But when I started to think about a scone that would be great for book club, I realized I wanted something updated. First, Hayes' recipes were definitely twentieth-century sized, with 4 or 4 1/2 cups of flour and other grains yielding eight scones—they were more of a meal than an item on a buffet table. The recipes relied either on butter (delicious, though heavy) or vegetable shortening (neither tasty nor very good for you). The recipes were loaded with eggs, cream, half and half, and sugar as well: totally authentic, but not exactly on par with the healthier tastes of the 2020s. Thus, I set out to make a scone that my book club members would love: something very light and a little sweet and incredibly moist. But something that was still definitely a European-style scone: a triangle of bread raised with baking powder, just begging for a cup of tea to accompany it.

One of Hayes' original recipes was for a blueberry scone. I never actually made it because the recipe involved making scone dough and then folding fresh blueberries into it. Frankly, it sounded like a mess to me. But when trying to imagine a vegan scone that would stay moist, fresh fruit sounded like a brilliant solution if I could streamline the process—which I did. For the liquid, I decided on oat milk, which has a great mouthfeel and a naturally sweet flavor. Then I added some much-needed zing with lemon, a blueberry's best friend. When I came to the shortening element, I tried a number of vegan butter substitutes, like coconut oil and applesauce. But what seemed to work and taste best was a plant-based mixture with a butter flavor. The brand most widely available is Earth Balance, but there are many other "buttery" spreads as well. Any of them should work, provided you make the time to chill the dough thoroughly before baking and move the baking trays directly from the refrigerator to the oven. That, along with the hot oven temperature, will help them keep their lovely triangular shape.

One final note: although they are now cultivated in the British Isles, blueberries are native to North America. Their European cousins, bilberries, would be more authentic. But I've never seen them available fresh in my part of the Northeast US. Dried bilberries are available, but they wouldn't add the same moistness, and they're crazy expensive. So, I'd stick with the anachronistic blueberries for this recipe.

Equipment you will need: a pastry blender; parchment paper; sifter, or a medium-mesh strainer

Another thing you'll need: Enough room in the refrigerator to store your baking sheets for an hour

Equipment that would be nice: a bench scraper

Yield: 16 small scones

Ingredients:

4 cups all-purpose flour, plus more for kneading
2 T vegan sugar*
4 t baking powder
1/2 t cream of tartar
1/4 t table salt
12 T (6 oz) chilled vegan buttery spread (straight from the refrigerator)
2 lemons
6 oz fresh blueberries
1 1/4–1 1/2 c unsweetened oat milk
1 T limoncello (optional)
1 c vegan powdered sugar*

1. Line 2 baking sheets with parchment paper.
2. Add the flour, sugar, baking powder, cream of tartar, and salt to a large bowl. Whisk to combine.
3. Cut the buttery spread into small pieces and scatter over the dry ingredients in the bowl. Using a pastry blender, cut the spread into the dry ingredients until it's evenly distributed, with no pieces of spread larger than a pea remaining. The mixture will feel moist to the touch. (Alternatively, you can use two knives to work the spread into the dry ingredients, crossing them and pulling them apart. I find this method takes a long time and results in a less even distribution of the shortening, but if your technique is better than mine, it will work just as well.) Set the bowl aside.

4. Zest both lemons, dividing the zest evenly into 2 small bowls. Juice both lemons (you should have about 5–6 T of lemon juice) and set aside.
5. Add one-half of the zest to the mixture in the bowl. Mix to combine.
6. Check over the blueberries and remove any stems. Add the blueberries to the bowl, then gently fold them into the mixture using a rubber spatula.
7. Add 2 T of the lemon juice to the oat milk. Slowly pour the oat milk mixture over the ingredients in the bowl, then gently fold a few times to moisten the mixture, forming a soft but still ragged dough. If the dough won't hold together, add more oat milk a tablespoon at a time. But don't worry that it's not uniform at this point—some dry areas are normal.
8. Sprinkle a few tablespoons of flour on a work surface. Turn the dough onto the work surface and then pull it together gently into a rounded heap, gently patting the sides and top gently and rotating a 1/4-turn a couple of times until you have a loose disk. Knead by patting the top gently to flatten and fold one half over the other. Repeat the process four or five times until the dough comes together into a firm disc. (You may need to sprinkle a bit more flour if the dough is sticking but try not to overdo it.)
9. Divide the disc into 4 even pieces with a knife or a bench scraper. Gently pat and rotate each piece until you have 4 even discs. (You can lightly roll a rolling pin over the discs to make them look more uniform.) Cut each of the discs in half, then in half again, to form 4 triangles. Place 8 triangles, about two inches apart, on each of the baking

sheets. Cover the sheets with plastic wrap and put the sheets into the refrigerator for about an hour.

10. Preheat the oven to 425 degrees. Move the scones directly from the refrigerator to the oven, placing each sheet on its own rack. Bake the scones for 13–15 minutes, or until golden brown, rotating the baking sheets upper to lower and front to back, at about 7 minutes. Remove the scones to a cooling rack.

11. When the scones are cool, make the glaze. Sift the powdered sugar into a medium bowl. Add the remaining lemon zest to the sugar and stir to combine. Add the limoncello, if using, and whisk into the powdered sugar mixture. Then add the remaining lemon juice, tablespoon by tablespoon, until you have a pourable glaze, about the consistency of honey. If you run out of lemon juice, you can add water, a tablespoon at a time.

12. Dip the top of each scone in the lemon glaze, letting excess drip back into bowl. Return to the rack to let the glaze harden.

13. Serve with jam or vegan chocolate-hazelnut spread.

*Note: Not all brands of sugar are vegan, seeing as some use bone char in the refining process. If having the recipe turn out vegan is critical, it's important to seek out vegan brands. Both vegan and non-vegan brands of sugar will work in this recipe, however.

Tea Sandwiches

———

Nothing was more eagerly anticipated (or more disappointing) than my first "tea." I'm not exactly sure what I was expecting. Based on movies set in the Regency or Victorian era, I expected something regal. The Queen? A string quartet playing in the background, maybe? But when my hosts put down some bar food (they ran a pub, so that made sense) and a tray of "biscuits"—which I was pretty sure were cookies—and a couple of mugs of tea, along with beer, sodas, and milk, on the coffee table in front of the telly so we could all watch *Coronation Street*, I'm going to admit, it was a bummer.

What I didn't know then was that "tea" wasn't the same as "high tea." Tea was just another name for supper in Slough, the London suburb where I was an exchange student. The disappointment soon passed—I had almost twenty years of *Coronation Street* to catch up on, after all. And there was something kind of fun about calling the biggest meal of the day by another name. Almost as fun as calling the trunk of the car the "boot" or the elevator the "lift."

Fast forward thirty-five years or so, and I'd learned a lot about "high tea" and had even had the experience a couple of times. So, I was super excited to take my daughter Eleanor to a famous Marylebone hotel in London for their version on her first trip to London. We made reservations for high tea at a spot listed by a famous travel magazine as having one of the best traditional high teas in the city. We got all dressed up, got in a cab, and finally arrived in the room of my original fantasy: a huge space with pink walls and an enormous flower display at the entrance.

There were dozens of tables clad in white tablecloths, all holding gleaming crystal, silver, and china. We were shown to a table with banquette seating, perfect so we could sit side-by-side and watch the action in the room. Our waitress was lovely and enthusiastic, suggesting a bright pink hibiscus tea for my dubious daughter and a mild Assam blend for me. (Why thank you very much, I will have a glass of bubbly as well!) Finally, the three-tiered tower of deliciousness arrived at the table with great ceremony. There was a tray of mixed finger sandwiches, another tray of scones, and another topped with miniature desserts and pastries. Watching Ellie's eyes grow round and her mouth form an "O" when the goodies were set down was a priceless motherhood moment.

Another one came a few moments later, with the very grossed out, pained look on her face after she bit into her first cucumber sandwich. I could tell getting the bite down was a struggle, but she did it—and then discreetly put the rest of the sandwich on the corner of her plate. I winked an approval for her to move onto the scones, lemon curd, and clotted cream, and the afternoon was saved.

Of course, I had to try the culprit morsel myself. I wasn't totally grossed out. But she had a point. The sandwich looked prim and pretty, but the bread was actually kind of wet. The cucumber was soft, rather than snappy. The butter was rich and delicious, but there wasn't enough bitterness or crunch to provide contrast. The rest of our tea was scrumptious, and "high tea" even went on to become a special occasion meal at our house. But I left there wondering what was missing. Things like cucumber sandwiches usually become staples for a reason. So, once I got home, I played around with the recipe until a cucumber sandwich was something everyone in our house looked forward to. The secret was simple—it just takes some planning.

And there's no need to wait for high tea—or book club—to make them. Cucumber sandwiches can be the basis of an easy vegetarian meal in summer when it's too hot to consider turning the oven on. They're also awesome in a picnic basket because, as I found out, they don't get soggy if you make them right. And cucumbers are just the beginning. Chefs all over the world are getting creative with their tea sandwiches, and so can you!

What I'm providing for you is a method of making a tea sandwich, and a few sample fillings. You can make them plain (leave the crusts on) or fancy (trim the crusts off). I've included my riff on the traditional cucumber sandwich, as well as a curried chicken and currant that would feel right at home on a Regency tea tray. There's also a set of combinations that come directly from your deli counter, olive bar, and condiment aisle and come together in a snap, but still deliver the tastes of an afternoon at Netherfield.

TO MAKE A TEA SANDWICH

Yield: 16 small sandwich triangles or 12 fingers (can be multiplied or divided)

Equipment you will need: plastic wrap; paper towels; a cutting board

Equipment that would be nice: an offset spatula; a sturdy, serrated bread knife

Ingredients:

8 slices thin-sliced, sturdy white bread, such as Pepperidge Farm's Very Thin Enriched White Bread
1 stick of quality unsalted butter, such as Kerrygold, at room temperature
Salt and pepper, to taste

1. "Open" two consecutive pieces of bread from the package like a book.
2. Spread the top of each bread slice with a thin layer of butter, using an offset spatula if possible to make it perfectly smooth. You want just enough so you don't see the bread peeking through.
3. Place each piece of bread in the middle of a piece of plastic wrap and fold the plastic wrap gently over the buttered side. Place the wrapped bread slices in the refrigerator for at least an hour, until the butter is quite firm. If you're not going to trim the crusts, keep the pairs together so you know which two will fit perfectly together.
4. If you plan to trim the crusts, stack two slices of bread on a cutting board and carefully trim the edges with a

serrated bread knife. I recommend trimming the crusts if you plan to make finger sandwiches—it matters less for the traditional triangular tea sandwich shape. (I just throw them in the food processor, pulse a few times, and throw them on a baking sheet at 250 degrees until they are dried out. Voila—fresh buttered bread crumbs!)

5. Lightly salt and pepper the buttered bread slices. Working as quickly as possible, layer the sandwich ingredients on one piece of bread, leaving a small border so the ingredients don't extend beyond the edge.

6. Place the other piece of bread on top of the sandwich and press gently to stabilize. Wrap the completed sandwich in plastic wrap—not so tightly that the filling squeezes out or the bread loses its shape, but with enough pressure so the ingredients are held together firmly. Put the sandwich back in the refrigerator and repeat with the other 3 sandwiches.

7. Refrigerate for at least an hour, and for up to 24 hours.

8. When ready to serve, unwrap each sandwich and place on a cutting board. For traditional tea sandwiches, cut the sandwich in half from the upper left corner to the bottom right corner with a serrated knife using a "sawing" motion so you don't mash the bread together and ruin the layered effect. Wipe the blade clean using the paper towel. Rotate each sandwich so the longest edge is toward the bottom of the cutting board. Cut each triangle in half from the top point to the center of the longest side, wiping the knife clean after each cut.

9. For finger sandwiches, lay the sandwich on the board and cut in thirds vertically, using the same sawing technique described above, wiping the knife after each cut.

10. Arrange sandwiches side-by-side on a platter with bread touching so the filling layers are visible. Serve immediately.

CUCUMBER SANDWICH FILLING

Equipment you will need: a colander; a clean, lint-free cotton or linen tea towel (terry cloth and microfiber towels will not work properly)

Equipment that would be nice: a mandolin slicer

Ingredients:

6 mini cucumbers or 1 large seedless cucumber
2 1/2 t salt, divided
8 ounces whipped cream cheese, such as Temp Tee
1/4 c chopped fresh dill
2 T chopped fresh tarragon
5–10 fresh chives, thinly sliced
Zest of 1 lemon
1/4 t ground white pepper
Watercress or baby arugula (optional)

1. An hour before you plan to put the sandwiches together, prepare the cucumbers. Using a mandolin (or your legendary knife skills), cut the cucumbers into very thin slices.
2. Toss the slices into the colander, sprinkle with 2 t table salt, and allow to sweat for about an hour. Place a plate or a bowl under the colander to catch any juices.
3. Bring the colander to the sink and discard any accumulated cucumber juice from the plate. Rinse the cucumber slices thoroughly under cool running water.

4. Spread the tea towel out on a work surface and dump the cucumber slices in the center. Gather up the corners of the tea towel above the cucumbers and bring the towel over the sink. Push the cucumbers together in the bottom of the tea towel, and then slowly twist the towel so that it tightens around the cucumbers, releasing as much of the juice as possible—this is going to keep your sandwich from going soggy in the fridge. When most of the water has been released, remove the cucumbers from the towel and place on a platter or baking sheet lined with paper towels.

5. In a separate bowl, mix together the cream cheese, dill, tarragon, chives, lemon zest, 1/2 t salt, and white pepper. Mix thoroughly. Taste for salt and pepper and adjust, if necessary. Refrigerate until ready to layer sandwich (Step 5, To Make a Tea Sandwich, above).

6. Layer 1/4 of the cream cheese mixture on top of the bread, smoothing out with an offset spatula if possible. Layer cucumber pieces on the cream cheese, pushing them very gently into the cream cheese, and overlapping so there are no gaps in the layer. Top the cucumbers with a layer of watercress or arugula, if using.

7. Continue with Step 6, **To Make a Tea Sandwich**, at the beginning of this section.

CURRIED CHICKEN FILLING

Equipment you will need: a small saucepan with a tight-fitting lid; an instant-read thermometer

Equipment that would be nice: a Microplane grater

Ingredients:

2 boneless, skinless chicken breasts
1 c white wine
1 t stock base, such as Better Than Bouillon, or 1 bouillon cube
1 small yellow onion, peeled and sliced into 1/2-inch slices
4 cloves garlic, peeled
1 bay leaf
6 peppercorns
3 allspice berries (optional)
1 T salt, divided
3 T mayonnaise
2 t white wine vinegar
1 1/2 t curry powder
1 t grated fresh ginger
1/4 c currants
1 stalk celery, finely chopped, leaves included
3 T Greek yogurt, labne, or yogurt cheese*
2 T prepared mango chutney, such as Patak's

1. First, poach the chicken breasts. Add two cups water to a lidded saucepan large enough to hold both chicken breasts without overlapping. Add the wine, stock base, onion slices, garlic, peppercorns, allspice berries, bay leaf, and 2 t salt to the pan. Bring to a boil over medium heat, then reduce to a simmer. Cover the pan to reduce evaporation and cook for 15 minutes.

2. Add the chicken breasts to the simmering stock, cover the pan, and slowly simmer chicken breasts, checking the temperature beginning at 5 minutes (timing will vary widely based on the size of your chicken breasts), until they reach an internal temperature of 160 degrees, then

turn off the heat, leaving the chicken in the poaching liquid for another 5 minutes. This will gently bring the temperature up to 165 degrees without the chicken drying out. At 165 degrees, remove from the poaching liquid to a plate and allow to cool completely. Once cool, place the chicken breasts in a covered container or cover in plastic wrap and refrigerate. This can be done up to 24 hours in advance.

3. When you're ready to put the sandwiches together (Step 5, To Make a Tea Sandwich, above), place the mayonnaise, vinegar, and 1/2 t salt in a small bowl.

4. Remove the chicken from the refrigerator and chop it finely (about 1/4-inch pieces)—the small size will make the sandwiches daintier—and much easier to cut—later. Add the chicken to a medium mixing bowl.

5. Fold the mayonnaise mixture into the chicken, then fold in the currants and celery. Taste for salt and adjust seasoning if necessary.

6. If the brand of chutney you are using contains large pieces of fruit, remove them from the jam and mince them. In a small bowl, mix together the yogurt and chutney. Salt to taste.

7. Remove two pieces of bread from the refrigerator. Layer one piece of bread with the chicken salad and the other with the yogurt mixture. Gently press the two sides together.

8. Continue with Step 6, **To Make a Tea Sandwich**, above.

OTHER TEA SANDWICH COMBINATIONS

Once you have the formula down, almost anything can be a tea sandwich; just follow the steps described in **To Make a Tea Sandwich**, listed above. If you're a person with a lot of leftovers around, you can approach your refrigerator like a basket from "Chopped." That hard-boiled egg would make a nice layer. You could swap out the cucumber in the cucumber sandwich for that smoked salmon leftover from brunch. Cheddar, caramelized onions, and marmalade make a surprisingly tangy sandwich filling. Some baby spinach or arugula would pair beautifully with that leftover herbed cheese spread—just let it soften on the counter before spreading on the bread.

If you're willing to make a trip to the grocery store before book club meets, there are even more possibilities. Here are some delicious pairings that will look pretty on the tea tray— no cooking required:

- Shaved roast beef + parsley + horseradish mayo
- Thinly sliced tavern ham + cheddar cheese + apple butter
- Egg salad + dried tomatoes + watercress

A Model Trifle

———

I am a big fan of giving actual presents for weddings, usually something for the kitchen. I know many couples would like cash to put toward a down payment for a house or to defer honeymoon expenses. But those gifts don't have much impact. I received a lot of very generous gifts when I got married, but the ones I am still able to use thirty years later are precious, a frequent reminder that I was very important to someone. I still adore using the Villeroy & Boch gratin dishes my high school English teacher, Patty Dose, gave me when I got married—that gift has been part of every Thanksgiving and Christmas meal I've cooked since the 1990s. I still love snuggling under the intarsia blanket Beryl McLaughlin, Lee's grandmother, knitted for us. And because Rita and Jim Gleason gave us a beautiful bowl edged with dolphins for a wedding present, I decided trifle was going to become part of my dessert repertoire.

I started by asking some English and Irish friends if they had a trifle recipe they could share. But the responses were pretty non-committal. "It's just something my gran makes." "I love when it's on the menu, but I don't really make it myself." It didn't seem like a "great baker" thing. As I started to read recipes, it became clear that trifle is just layers of whatever the cook likes.

There are a few constants: two cakey layers, a jammy layer, a custardy layer, and a creamy layer. But after that, it was all over the place. Some had fruit; others didn't. Dried fruits, nuts, and chocolate chips made appearances, but I wasn't convinced. Some recipes called for elaborate sponges, long-cooking jams, and homemade creme patissiere. Others just fell back on store-bought lady fingers. It was all pretty confusing and possibly the kind of thing you'd relegate to "once-a-year" status if you were trying to make it all from scratch. I was looking for a model I could make easily—and often.

Then I remembered Bird's custard powder—it's basically the British answer to a box of Jell-O pudding. Depending on the amount of milk used, you can either get it to set into a firm custard or leave it relatively thin, like a crème anglaise. I remembered it was a teatime feature during my foreign exchange days in England. It was super easy to make, and the powder was widely available in the US. And not a fussy egg in sight. Creamy layer accomplished.

Next, I looked for a reliable cake layer. I tried the ubiquitous angel food cakes available to accompany summer fruits at most grocery stores, but found they got mushy. I tried ladyfingers, but they were not very substantial and fell apart when serving, leaving a crumby mess in the bowl. Walking through the freezer aisle one day, I hit on it: an all-butter pound cake that nobody doesn't like! Thawed and cut into cubes, its firm texture would soak up jam or custard, but not disintegrate in the process. Over the years, I've tried a bunch of different cake layers in my trifle and have used the model to salvage a couple of cakes that were too dry or wouldn't release well from the pan (including one infused with rosewater to celebrate a Penn State appearance in the Rose Bowl). That withstanding, the frozen pound cake remains a favorite for taste, texture, and pure accessibility.

When it came to the jam layer, I decided to splurge. The quintessential British jam is Tiptree's Little Scarlet, a strawberry jam so intense and addictive that my daughters refer to it as "the crack of jellies." It adds a strong tart-but-sweet note to the trifle. According to brand enthusiast Zahra Pettican, writing in *Bon Appétit* magazine, the jam is made of tiny strawberries five times as sweet and flavorful as the big ones cultivated by industrial farms. Just warm it up, pour it over, and let it do its magic. If the steep price of Little Scarlet is off-putting (totally reasonable), or it's not available in your area, you can use any high-quality jam. And if strawberries aren't your jam (see what I did there?), no problem. Any flavor will work here. This is just a model. Change it with the season, the holiday, or your mood.

One place where I don't mess around is the creamy layer. Nothing is better than real whipped cream—absolutely nothing. I add a little vanilla. Maybe some cinnamon if I'm going for an autumn vibe. No sugar, because I don't need it—but if you like it sweet, go ahead and add a teaspoon or two.

That said, it would be perfectly possible to make a vegan version of this. Vegan cupcakes or almond cake would make a fine cakey layer. Tiptree jams are vegan-friendly, as is Bird's

Custard—just reconstitute it with a form of plant-based milk, such as soy or oat. A combination of vegan chocolate cake, cherry jam, and almond milk custard would be a heavenly ode to a Black Forest cake! Finally, top with a plant-based whipped cream substitute. There are plenty of recipes online, but well-stocked supermarkets carry some as well. Ready Whip now makes an almond milk cream if you're in a hurry!

Equipment you will need: any clear bowl—to show off your lovely layers (a 3- or 4-quart bowl, or several individual clear ramekins or small Mason jars, if desired); a serrated knife

Equipment that would be nice: a trifle bowl; a hand mixer or standing mixer

Ingredients:

1 16-oz frozen all-butter pound cake, thawed, or the equivalent amount of any cake you choose
1/2 c sherry, Madeira, or fruit brandy, such as Poire William (optional)
3 cups fruit or berries (such as strawberries, blueberries, kiwis, cherries, peaches, or bananas, or any combination)
Lemon juice, if using fruit that easily oxidizes (good for preventing fruits like apples and peaches from turning brown)
1 8 oz jar of quality jam
2 T Bird's custard powder
2 c whole milk
2–4 T sugar, divided
1 c heavy cream
2 t vanilla extract

1. Put the jam in a small saucepan over low heat. Stir occasionally until it's completely melted—the jam should be completely liquid and will coat a spoon. Let cool.
2. Using a serrated knife, cut the cake into 1-inch cubes. Place half the cubes in the bottom of the bowl you will be serving it in (or divide half among individual serving bowls).
3. Sprinkle half the sherry over the cake cubes, if using.
4. If using fruit that quickly turns brown after peeling, like peaches or bananas, toss with lemon juice. Scatter 1/2 the fruit over the cake, making sure some of it is against the glass. Halved strawberries look very attractive here, as do kiwi and banana slices. This is your trifle, however, so use your imagination.
5. Pour the warm jam over the cake and fruit layer, spreading it out to make sure some of it reaches the bowl edge— it adds to the drama.
6. Repeat the cake, sherry, and fruit layers.
7. Using the custard powder, 2 T sugar, and the milk, make the custard according to the package directions. Allow to cool slightly, then pour over the cake and fruit, spreading to make sure all of the cake is covered and that the custard spreads to the edge. Cover the bowl with plastic wrap and allow to set in the refrigerator for at least 2 hours, and up to 24 hours.
8. An hour before you are ready to serve, chill a mixing bowl or the bowl of a standing mixer in the refrigerator.
9. Right before serving, pull the bowl from the refrigerator and add the heavy cream, vanilla, and remaining sugar, if using. Using the mixer or the whisk attachment of a standing mixer, whip the cream until medium peaks form. When the beater or whisk is pulled straight up out

of the bowl, peaks should stand up, but the tips will fold over. This can take anywhere from a minute to a few minutes, depending on the speed of your mixer. Do not overbeat.

10. Remove the plastic wrap from the trifle. Scrape the whipped cream on top and smooth to make an even layer.

11. Garnish with extra fruit or cinnamon, if you wish.

Taking Book Club to the Next Level: Pride and Prejudice

BEVERAGES TO OFFER:

Non-alcoholic drinks: Tea, coffee, and hot chocolate would have been at home on any Regency tea table. While all would have been served with sugar and cream, coconut milk or oat milk would make fantastic vegan substitutes—just remember to combine with vegan sugar and chocolate. Lemonade was a popular party offering—just make sure that it's "cloudy" or non-carbonated lemonade. Although common today in England, carbonated lemonade didn't appear until well after the Regency period.

Alcoholic drinks: Because of the importance of fortified wine to the Regency pantry, offering sherry, port, Madeira, or a cocktail featuring one of them would be a solid choice. Vinoble, an international fortified wine association, highlights a number of cocktail recipes on their website. But, according to *Jane Austen's World*—the de facto authority on all things Austen—war and social conditions on the European continent made traditional grape-based wines very expensive during the Regency period, and English households during the time turned to local fruits to make their own wines. Elder wine, made from elderberries, was a particular favorite. There's a bit of a renaissance in the fruit wine sector in the US at the moment, according to the alcoholic beverage blog *Tasting Table*. Including a cherry wine from the Midwest or an apple wine from New England would certainly evoke the spirit of the time.

MUSIC TO PLAY:

With all the movie and television versions of Jane Austen's novels, it's not difficult to find soundtrack albums that can provide a suitable backdrop for your *Pride and Prejudice* discussion—all of which can be found on popular streaming services such as Spotify or Amazon Music. The soundtrack for the blockbuster mini-series *Bridgerton* features covers of popular tunes covered in the Regency style—it's fun trying to guess the original tunes and artists. But for all things Regency music and dance, head over to regencydances.org, the brainchild of Garth Notley, where you'll find videos of Regency dance organizations performing cotillions, quadrilles, and country dances—but not very many waltzes. They've also curated a set of six albums of accurate period music. Some of the albums include dance notations, in case your club members are willing to try their hand at one of the popular figure dances from the time. You'll even find a section on ballroom etiquette—for goodness' sake, no hissing during the country dances, if you please!

TABLESCAPES:

According to Sarah Nichols, writing for the Carnegie Museum of Art's magazine, "In the 18th century, as before and since, the objects used to lay a table spoke volumes about the host's standing in society." So, this is the time to bring out the china, silver, and crystal that's been gathering dust in the sideboard since 2019. During the Regency era, large elegant dinners were set out in a series of "removes," usually three separate courses made up of many different dishes. But presenting all the elements of the meal together, aside from dessert, would have been common for smaller family dinners. Linen tablecloths are *de rigueur*, but according to AC Silver silversmith's blog, napkins were not always in fashion during the period. What were popular were covered tureens, for keeping food warm, and multi-armed epergnes, or centerpieces, that held everything from fruit to saltshakers to pickles. While vintage pieces can be found for as much as $70,000 in antique stores, you can recreate the look by using inexpensive multi-tiered trays.

On Champagne, Strawberries, and Shakespeare

———

I took my first trip abroad with seven other students from Smithtown High School East, with a lone English teacher, Bob Ranieri, to keep us in line. Each politically incorrect Smithtown Indian was paired with the family of a student from our sister school in Slough, England, of all places. Upon reflection, it's hard to believe that my conservative, overprotective cop of a father let me get on a plane and spend the summer between my junior and senior years of high school in another country. But the principal of the school, Roger Sullivan, even made an effort to call my dad and tell him how good the trip would look on my college applications. I'm not sure if it was my constant begging or the fact that one of my best friends had permission to go that finally swayed them, but somehow, my folks scraped together the money and sent me across the pond.

It probably wasn't a good sign that instead of her parents, the student I was paired with showed up—late—in her boyfriend's Mini Cooper, cramming my huge suitcase in the back seat with me for the long ride to her family's pub on the outskirts of town. She dropped me off with her mum and dad for tea and departed immediately. As it turned out, she was in a very different place when I arrived in England than she'd been when she signed up to host me, and she was no longer interested in making a connection with anyone but her "Jimmykins" (barf). Away from home for the first time, and not even within walking distance of the rest of my US crew, I was so miserable after a week that I phoned the one person I knew in all of England and cried my heart out to my mom's friend Sylvia.

When I first met Sylvia, I thought she was like something out of a movie—or maybe a British comedy sketch. Sylvia's family came into the lives of my family by way of my mom's friend Rita, who met Sylvia, Colin, and their son Peter while on sabbatical in Surrey. I remember being introduced to them years later at a barbeque when I was about thirteen years old. They were all perfectly dressed in sensible but clearly expensive, perfectly tailored clothes that looked like they wouldn't have dared wrinkle. Their accents were clipped and uppercrusty. They chatted about things like tennis, travel (Colin worked for the old British Overseas Air Company, and they'd been *everywhere*), and literature. They drank gin and tonics without ice. And no matter what the topic, Sylvia had the perfect anecdote. She was fancy and cultured—everything a cop's kid from Long Island thought it would be cool to be. I simply adored her.

Sylvia listened to my pathetic story of teenage abandonment, paused for a moment, and said, "Right. Be ready at 9 a.m. on Saturday morning. Colin will be picking you up directly."

"I don't think I'm allowed to go anywhere without my group, Sylvia."

"Now, you just let me worry about that," Sylvia chimed, with the sort of British cheerful maternal fortitude that my daughters' generation might identify with Molly Weasley. "We can't have our girl getting the wrong idea about England, can we?"

Apparently, some phone calls were made. And in the 1980s, overseas calls were *expensive*. In the end, Sylvia got permission to take me on weekends when my group didn't have any programming planned. So, on Saturday at 9 a.m., I was standing outside the door, hugging Sylvia's husband Colin, and hopping into the car with all the expectation of, say, Persephone finally sprung from the Underworld.

Sylvia's plan to save my holiday was absolutely inspired. When I arrived, there was tea and buttery shortbread to chat over (Food!). Then, we went for a ramble through a maze at Hampton Courts, a favorite palace of King Henry VIII (History!). And instead of heading home for dinner, Sylvia grabbed a picnic hamper, bundled us all into the car, and surprised me with an open-air performance of *A Midsummer Night's Dream* (Literature!) There were tiny, crustless sandwich triangles. Juicy strawberries dipped in chocolate. White asparagus we were permitted to hold in our hands and dip into herby green dressing because we were "in the outdoors, after all." And there was my first glass of champagne

(Booze! Bubbles!). As the stars came out and the stage lights came on, I lay back on the blanket, my head propped up with pillows, and realized I was having one of the best days of my sixteen-year-old life.

Now looking back on more than forty years at that long-ago picnic, I realize I wasn't wrong. My whole trip was saved by strawberries, champagne, and Shakespeare—and by Sylvia, who was determined to share the best of her culture with an Irish-American teenager that she hardly knew. The play, after all, was the thing.

A TALE WITH A TWIST FROM SPAIN

Photo credit: Lee Ahern

The Book Recommendation: Pepita Jiménez

———

A story told in letters immediately draws me into the characters' world. There's something so intimate about "reading over the shoulder" of the characters, experiencing their correspondence along with them. But epistolary novels can also be disconcerting for the reader—we can never be entirely sure about the reliability of the communications we're reading. I imagine authors must struggle with being authentic in more than one voice at a time and having complete sympathy with multiple characters. Every change in perspective is a turning point. It's a high-risk, high-reward strategy, hardly noticeable when it's done well, and disastrous when it's handled poorly. This is one reason I think *Pepita Jiménez* would be such a fascinating and rewarding choice for a book club read.

Despite its title, the novel centers around a young seminarian, Don Luis de Vargas, who has been raised by his uncle, the

Dean of a Cathedral School. The preface informs the reader that the text was found among the Dean's papers after his death, in three distinct parts (all in the Dean's handwriting)—but we are never told who it is that has gone on to "publish" the Dean's notes. The three parts are labeled "Letters from My Nephew," which consists of dated excerpts from Don Luis' letters to his uncle; "Paralipomena," in which the Dean (presumably) relays information from another source or sources; and "Letters from My Brother," an epilogue that brings the multiple threads of the story together.

Pepita Jiménez is probably the best-known novel by Juan Valera, a Spanish career diplomat posted at various times throughout his long career in Germany, Brazil, Russia, Austria, and the United States. Born in 1824, Valera lived through the waning days of Spain's colonial empire. Like many skilled diplomats, Valera was deployed when and where his skills were needed. In between assignments, he was part of Madrid's literary and intellectual scene. It was during a lull from diplomacy that he wrote *Pepita Jiménez*, his most famous novel.

When we meet Don Luis, he is on a trip to visit his father, Don Pedro, a wealthy gentleman farmer, before taking his final vows and becoming a Catholic priest. Having accumulated land and other assets, Don Pedro decides that since he is losing his heir to the Church, he will need to marry again. He sets his sights on the beautiful twenty-year-old widow Pepita Jiménez. Poor Pepita was married off by her domineering mother to an eighty-year-old uncle as a means of securing the girl's future, and his death three years prior to the beginning of the action has left her a merry widow indeed. While it's clear she would be a fantastic catch and had already received plenty of offers, Pepita doesn't seem inclined to remarry. Seminarian Don Luis meets Pepita as a prospective stepmother—but his letters to his uncle increasingly focus on the charming Pepita and chronicle a deepening crisis in vocation.

Pepita is rendered from three different perspectives. First, from Don Luis, who finds himself drawn to her despite his desire to follow in the paths of the saints. Having grown up in a seminary, he knows very little about women. So, one of the central explorations of the novel is passion, from both a clerical and a secular perspective. Is the priesthood a higher calling than marriage? Is loving a woman the same thing as giving in to temptation? The epistolary device shows us his inner struggle, leaving us with a vivid, though incomplete, picture of the title character.

But then the perspective shifts—and Pepita is redrawn in the "Paralipomena" section of the novel. According to Merriam-Webster, paralipomena can be defined as "things passed over but added as a supplement." So, Valera, through the Dean, indicates this information is somehow secondary to the letters. But why? And who is the mysterious source? The shift gives us a new Pepita—more assertive, more direct, more determined. Is she the source herself? Is it her faithful servant, Antoñona? Someone else entirely? In this section, the reader finally sees her version of events, and that, in turn, forces us to reassess what we know about Don Luis, his father Don Pedro, and even the Dean who's collecting the tale.

Our final rendition of Pepita comes from snippets gleaned from Don Pedro's letters to his brother, which form an epilogue to the story (although the Dean indicates in the text that no epilogue is necessary). The notes are cheerful and positive—very much the correspondence of an enthusiastic parent who can't help but brag about their cherished family. There is certainly no hint of a spurned potential husband—no regret, and certainly no acrimony. And the reader is very much left to wonder, "Were we had? And if we were, by whom?"

Although *Pepita Jiménez* is considered one of Spain's classic novels, most Americans who have read it probably encountered it in Spanish class. And the simple descriptions and declarative sentences indeed make it a fitting choice for one's first novel in a second language. There are several good translations, and at least one is bilingual, so readers interested in practicing their Spanish can first read each paragraph in the original language and then refer to the translation. Like many literary classics, the novel has been turned into at least one motion picture. And there is even a lyric opera by Isaac Albeniz based on the novel. (A fantastic version, starring Spain's own Placido Domingo, was recorded in Madrid in the early 2000s.) But Pepita Jiménez is so much more than a first foreign language read.

I love recommending *Pepita Jiménez* to book clubs because I think it was a novel way ahead of its time—and one that deserves a second look. Sure, there are some long, philosophical passages that feel old-fashioned. And the intricacies of the Catholic faith may be a bit arcane for some readers. But the structure, realism, and subtle humor of the novel give it a distinctly modern feel. The shift in perspectives on the title character has an almost cinematographic edge. I adore how it gives us an epilogue, but not all the answers. And there's something so meta about how the author slyly makes a case for the veracity of his account, based on the fact that if he were lying, he would have come up with a far more interesting story. Valera's novel appears straightforward, but the characters play their cards close to their vests. When viewed in that manner, it makes sense that the novel was written by a skilled diplomat. In fact, focusing on text and subtext would be a great way to approach *Pepita Jiménez* as a book club.

The World of Pepita and Don Luis

———

Spain in the nineteenth century can be summed up in a word: chaos. And, interestingly enough, career diplomat Juan Valera, the author of *Pepita Jiménez*, had a seat at the table for it all. This is why it's so interesting that Valera chose a bucolic setting for his fiction—far away from the political action. The world in which Valera lived his life was dominated by the clash of old powers unwilling to give up their roles, and upstart players on the world stage desperate to establish their power. A quiet life in the country must have seemed like a distant fantasy to Valera, and he chose to keep his characters buffered from—but not immune to—the realities of his world.

POLITICAL UNCERTAINTY AND THE END OF COLONIZATION

Although the year is unclear, we can assume that the novel takes place in the second half of the nineteenth century, sometime before the Cathedral Dean's notes were "found" and later published in 1874. Earlier in the century, Spain was overrun by Napoleon's army, which had long-term consequences for the decimated countryside. In fact, economic historians Leandro Prados de la Escosura and Carlos Santiago-Caballero call the Napoleonic invasion a "watershed moment" in Spanish economic history, in which a short-term crisis caused by the confiscation of livestock and the destruction of agricultural land was followed by a long-term redistribution of lands that the crown confiscated during its ongoing power struggle with the Catholic Church. Don Luis' father, Don Pedro, whose wealth is reported to be relatively new, may have benefitted from that redistribution.

By the middle of the nineteenth century, the powerful days of Spain's colonial past were declining. The Peninsular Wars, which ended in 1815, were followed in quick succession by revolutions throughout the Americas, led by Simon Bolivar and Jose San Marti. By the 1850s, Spain had relinquished its claims to all its American colonies, retaining only Cuba, Puerto Rico, and the Philippines, along with some smaller islands—those would later be claimed by a United States government taking up its own, problematic imperial course. In the mid-nineteenth century, the islands served to maintain some of Spain's trade with the Americas, but the loss of tax revenues and imports from South America and Mexico were more than just catastrophic for the crown. It also had repercussions for Spanish citizens, who had long used the military and bureaucracy as a means to improve family fortunes. We see this when Pepita's brother abandons the family, seeking to change their fortunes in the New World.

The Spanish government changed multiple times during the century, with Ferdinand VII deposed by Napoleon (who made his brother emperor), then restored to absolutism, then forced to live under constitutional law until the French put him back in absolute authority. And that was just between 1814 and 1833! The period of Valera's service was divided between monarchy and Republicanism—his appointment by so many different governments speaks both to his acumen and the limited power of the executive when faced with Spain's old and established bureaucracy. But living through the final years of the once-powerful Spanish Empire, especially at so close a vantage point, must have impacted Valera.

CATHOLICISM

Far more than the vagaries of changing governments, the day-to-day life of Pepita and Don Luis would have been impacted by the Catholic Church. Spain was a country where life's milestones—birth, coming-of-age, marriage, death—were all tied to the rites of the Catholic Church. The church seasons would have dictated times of fasting and feasts. In addition to birthdays, people would have celebrated their "name days," the Catholic feasts of the saints or biblical figures that every Catholic would have been named after. Pepita's status as a widow, still in mourning, was the result of a marriage, no matter how unlikely, that was blessed by the church. The vicar, a simple parish priest, is an important character in the novel, providing support and spiritual guidance to many of the characters.

Don Luis' ties to the church play a critical role in the novel, obviously. The text reveals that Don Luis' parents were not married, and as a young man, he clearly feels the sting of illegitimacy. By taking holy orders, Don Luis sees an opportunity to be reborn, and he dreams of living a saintly life of service, which he contrasts with the choices his father has made. Of course, Don Luis' theological training, inside the Cathedral school, was entirely theoretical. It's not until he meets Pepita that he starts to realize that the Catholic church's other acceptable path in adulthood—marriage—may have some merit after all.

AGRARIANISM

Well into the twentieth century, southern Spain remained an agrarian economy, dominated by two crops that grew plentifully in the Mediterranean climate: olives and grapes. Like Don Luis' father, Pepita is a prominent landholder. Her first polite discussions with Don Luis over lunch are about wine and olive oil production, where she shows herself to be knowledgeable in ways his seminary education has not addressed. Don Pedro underscores his son's educational shortcomings, urging him, for example, to learn to ride. That wouldn't be a vital skill for a budding cleric, but it would undoubtedly be necessary for someone about to become a wealthy landowner.

The geography of Spain has always driven its agriculture. The central, arid plateau where Madrid is located was always dependent on the more fertile areas to the north, east, and south for its very existence. *Pepita Jiménez* takes place in Andalusia—a sunny, fertile area, south of the central plain where the country's all-important olive production is located. Even today, taking the high-speed train between Madrid and

Sevilla, I found it astounding to see almost nothing but olive orchards for hours. In Pepita and Luis' time, that same trip would have taken days! Inside the southern Spanish cities, visitors would have encountered streets lined with Seville orange trees, originally planted during the Moorish occupation. Every town would have had standing markets, and there would have been regional market days for wholesalers. Other regions of Spain would have had other agricultural bases: peppers in Extremadura, livestock in the foothills of the Pyrenees. And the country's colonial ties would have made it one of the early European centers for New World crops, including tomatoes, peppers, and potatoes. So, despite the political chaos, rural towns like the one portrayed in *Pepita Jiménez* had the ability to sustain themselves, despite the direction of the political winds blowing from the capital.

Essential Elements
of Spanish Cuisine

—

The Iberian Peninsula is truly a crossroads between Europe and North Africa. Historically, its strategic location led to a series of conquests, each of them influencing the food that we now think of as "Spanish"—the Celts, the Greeks, the Romans, and the Moors all occupied parts of the peninsula at one time or another. But the varying terrains and ancient political boundaries have also influenced the country's food-ways. In a country with five recognized languages, Aranese, Basque, Catalan, Castillian, and Galician, it's not surprising that regional cuisines, or *cocinas*, played an essential role in food history. According to food historian Maria Jose Sevilla, author of *Delicioso!*, while agriculture came late to Iberia, its various sources have left it with the most diverse agrarian footprint of any European country.

But regional differences aside, the availability of abundant homegrown ingredients, its colonial past, along with the country's proximity to water and North Africa, have given it a unique flavor signature, recognizable around the globe.

SEAFOOD

Spain borders the Mediterranean Sea to the south and east, the Bay of Biscay to the north, and the North Atlantic to the west. Little wonder, then, that seafood has formed an important part of the Iberian diet since pre-historic times. During Pepita and Don Luis' time, Spanish fishermen would have provided a wide array of seafood to the markets daily, including clams (*almejas*), lobster (*langosta*), prawns (*gambas*), crabs (*buey de ma*r), octopus (*pulpo*), and squid (*calamar*), along with fish of all kinds. Paella, arguably Spain's most famous dish, often includes an array of seafood (*mariscos),* although versions featuring meat and vegetables are common in some parts of the country.

Iberians are said to have fished for cod (among other types) on the Grand Banks of North America, well before Colombus stepped foot in the Caribbean. Of course, without refrigeration, seafood has a short shelf life, so preserving the precious and abundant source of protein was a priority—which is why *bacalao*, cod preserved with salt, is a staple of the Spanish pantry. Bacalao is generally soaked and then added to stews and rice dishes, such as *arroz con bacalao*. Rehydrating bacalao is a multi-step process that can take up to two days, resulting in a firm, somewhat fishy, and surprisingly sweet protein. Bacalao a la Vizcaina— salted cod cooked with potatoes, tomatoes, and capers—is one of the signature dishes of Spain's Basque Country.

NORTH AFRICAN IMPORTS

When the Moors swept into the Iberian peninsula from North Africa in 711 CE, they brought with them a culture that far surpassed any in Europe at the time in terms of education and creature comforts. The beautiful Alhambra in Granada remains a tribute to the Moorish influence on Spanish culture, with running water, extraordinary tile and ironwork, and ornate gardens. My first Spanish teacher, Señora Ledesma, told me that almost any Spanish word starting with "al" is derived from Arabic, including la almohada (pillow), la almendra (almond), and el albaricoque (apricot).

But while the Moor's influence on the Spanish language is undeniable, their influence on cuisine was even more profound. Under Moorish control, Spain's agriculture was transformed, as administrators introduced land reforms and crops favored by the new residents.

It should come as no surprise that Spain's iconic *paella* is a rice dish. One of the first things the Umayyad rulers did was put the existing Roman system of aqueducts to work, creating the irrigation necessary for one crop in particular: rice. The irrigation system also enabled a dramatic expansion of Spain's olive orchards, and to this day, the country remains Europe's largest producer of olive oil.

Another significant Moorish introduction to southern Spain was bitter oranges. Cities such as Seville, Cordoba, and Granada saw the trees planted along major thoroughfares, where the Moorish citizens were able to enjoy their beautiful, fragrant blossoms in spring. The oranges—now known as "Seville oranges," despite their Asian origins—are too bitter to eat out of hand. (My husband tried to peel and eat one a few years ago on the street in Cordoba, but he couldn't get past the taste.) Their rinds were traditionally candied and either eaten by themselves or added to another Moorish innovation, the dessert course. But with enough sugar, Seville oranges become the main ingredient in orange marmalade, the UK's favorite toast topping. And according to Stephen Burgen, writing in *The Guardian*, most of Spain's Seville orange crop is now exported to England for that purpose. The rest serves as the flavoring for liqueurs such as Cointreau, and some is even used as biofuel, powering Seville's water treatment plant. That's a transplant that keeps on giving!

Another gift from the Moors can be found in the spice profile we associate with Spain. The most important addition was saffron, another component of paella, which the Moors cultivated extensively in southern Spain.

NEW WORLD INGREDIENTS

Beginning in the late fifteenth century, the Spanish, using their extensive naval and military might, lay claim to territories throughout the Americas and ultimately the Pacific. To say that European cuisine would never be the same is an understatement. Every "European" dish featuring potatoes, tomatoes, bell peppers, chili peppers, corn, chocolate, avocados, cherries, or sweet potatoes, to name only a few, owes its existence to New World crops. Because of Spain's pre-eminence in establishing trade routes to the Americas, the Spanish were among the first to have access to (and later cultivate) those crops at home. By the nineteenth century, these once "foreign" foods were staples of Spanish agriculture, mixing freely in Don Luis' description of Pepita's garden:

"The declivity at the end of the garden is full of walnut, hazel, fig, and other fruit trees; and in the level portion are beds planted with strawberries and vegetables, tomatoes, potatoes, beans and peppers. There is also a little flower-garden, with a great abundance of flowers, of the kinds most cultivated here."

PEPITA JIMÉNEZ: RECIPES FOR BOOK CLUB

"The entertainment, in the course
of which we were served with
refreshments, continued till twelve;
the refreshments were syrup served
in little cups, and afterward chocolate
with spongecake, and meringues
and sugared water."

Tortilla Española

——

It may seem strange that the most iconic of Spain's tapas can be whipped up with only four basic ingredients: potatoes, onions, eggs, and olive oil. But it's the simplicity and austerity of tortilla española that makes it so beloved—and maybe just a little intimidating. My baseline for any tapas bar is the quality of its tortilla. Because when a dish is that simple, everything comes down to technique and attention to detail. So, while at its heart, a tortilla is just a potato omelet, you need to take the time to make sure that each of the components is cooked and seasoned perfectly if you're going to wow your book club buddies with such simple fare.

Simple, yes, but tricky. I have eaten tortillas in fancy restaurants and hole-in-the-wall bars. I've sampled them in big cities and in tiny seaside towns. I can't find a pattern as to who makes the best tortillas. But it's easy to know when you get a good one. A well-made tortilla is a bite of heaven: creamy egg holding together perfectly seasoned potatoes, rich with olive oil. The potatoes must be fully cooked, with no hint of rawness, and have some caramelized, crunchy edges from frying.

Then there's the thorny question of additions. Is it okay to call something a tortilla española if it goes beyond those four foundational ingredients? The brilliant Spanish food writer Penelope Casas includes tuna and herbs in her tortilla. A *New York Times* recipe included both bell peppers and garlic, and it was greeted with more than thirty comments scoffing at the idea of "additions" to the already perfect tortilla—and the writer was working from a recipe by a Spanish chef! This may be a case where outsiders are more "purist" than the native cooks. I mean, who am I to tell a bunch of Catalans eating Truita amb Suc, a delicious spinach tortilla served with—heaven forbid—a red sauce, that they are doing it wrong?

Here's my quick take. If you're Spanish, a tortilla española is whatever your abuelita said it was, and you should just go with that. If, like me, you're not lucky enough to have an abuelita to pass down recipes, you can start with the classic recipe and make changes sparingly, as I have done here. I've turned out dozens of tortillas over the years, and my only addition is a healthy amount of parsley, which gives just a hint of freshness and a ton of good looks to the classic. If you're adding much more than that, save yourself the headache and tell everyone it's a "frittata." No one seems to get upset about messing with those.

Yield: 1 tortilla

Equipment you will need: an 8-inch non-stick skillet; a large baking sheet; a roll of paper towels; two large plates for flipping the pancake

Equipment that would be nice: a mandolin or v-slicer; a bird's nest strainer; an instant-read thermometer

Ingredients:

1 c extra-virgin olive oil
2 medium white or yellow onions
1 large or 2 small russet (baking) potatoes
5 free-range eggs
1 t kosher salt, plus more for seasoning the potatoes
1 t white pepper, plus more to season the potatoes
1/3 c parsley

1. Peel the onions, leaving the root end attached. If using a mandolin or v-slicer, attach the safety guard to the root end of one onion and slice into 1/8-inch slices. Repeat with the second onion. If using a chef's knife, cut the onions in half through the root, lay the onions flat on the cutting board, and slice thinly into half-moons. Discard the root ends.

2. Place the skillet over medium heat. Add 2 c olive oil to the pan. When the oil reaches about 210 degrees Fahrenheit, or when a slice of onion bubbles gently when added to the pan, add the onions to the oil a handful at a time, pressing them down when they begin to soften, then adding more. Poach the onions gently in the oil, stirring often, until they begin to caramelize, turning a rich, deep, golden color. This will take between 30 and 35 minutes. Adjust burner temperature as necessary to maintain a strong simmer. If you're using an instant-read thermometer, keep the oil temperature between 210 and 220 degrees. Place a couple of layers of paper towels on a baking sheet.

Using the bird's nest or a slotted spoon, lift the onions out of the oil, shaking gently to let as much oil as possible drain back into the pan. Spread the onions out on the paper towels to drain, then add to a large mixing bowl. Discard the paper towels.

3. While the onions are cooking, peel the potatoes. If using a mandolin or v-slicer, attach the safety guard to one end of the potatoes and slice each into 1/8-inch slices. If using a chef's knife, cut the potatoes in half length-wise, lay them flat on the cutting board, and slice thinly into half-moons.

4. Depending on how much the oil level in the skillet has come down, add another 1/2–1 c olive oil to the pan, bringing it back to the original oil level. Over medium heat, bring the oil temperature back to about 210–220 degrees Fahrenheit, or to the point where a slice of potato sizzles when it enters the pan. Carefully add about 1/3 of the potato slices to the pan. (I know many recipes suggest cooking all the potatoes at once, but I find they clump together if I do that, and the texture of the tortilla becomes uneven. Cooking the potatoes in batches does take more time, but it's worth it.)

5. Place a couple of layers of paper towels on the baking sheet. Using the bird's nest or a slotted spoon, When the first batch of potatoes are easily pierced with a knife and are starting to brown in spots, carefully remove the potatoes from the oil, shaking gently to let as much oil as possible drain back into the pan. Spread the potatoes out on the paper towels to drain, lightly salt and pepper them, then add to the onions in the large mixing bowl. Discard the paper towels. Repeat with the other 2 batches of potatoes. Drain the remaining oil from the pan, reserving in a heatproof bowl. Wipe out the pan with a paper towel.

6. While the last batch of potatoes is poaching, crack the eggs into a medium bowl. Whisk vigorously to incorporate the whites and the yolks completely. Chop the parsley.
7. Add the eggs, parsley, salt, and pepper to the bowl. Using a silicone spatula, gently incorporate all the ingredients, making sure the potatoes and onions are covered with egg. (Some potatoes are going to break, and that's just fine, but you don't want to mash them.)
8. Return the skillet to medium heat. Measure 2 T of the reserved olive oil and add it to the skillet. (Reserve the rest. Cool completely, strain, and store in the fridge. It's great for sautéing vegetables.) When the oil is hot and shimmering, add the potato and egg mixture to the pan, using a silicone spatula to spread it out evenly. Gently shake the pan back and forth the make sure the tortilla doesn't stick. Use the spatula to tighten up the edges of the tortilla. Reduce the heat to medium-low and cook until the edges are firm and the bottom is beginning to show spots of brown.
9. Now you're ready to flip! Carefully slide the tortilla out of the skillet and onto one of the plates. Quickly cover with the other plate and flip. Then, with the help of the spatula if necessary, slide the tortilla back into the skillet, uncooked side down. Continue cooking gently until the omelet is just cooked through—a skewer put through the center will be moist, but not eggy. Slide the tortilla onto a serving plate. Let cool for at least 15 minutes. The tortilla should be served warm or at room temperature, but not hot. It keeps for hours, so you can make it well ahead of serving.
10. Garnish with a bit more parsley, if desired. Cut into 8 wedges to serve.

Pinchos de Pollo y Vegetales

———

Spanish cuisine, as we know it today, was heavily influenced by the Iberian peninsula's Moorish occupation between 711 and 1492. When they came up from North Africa, the Moors brought with them spice combinations that most of us would think of as "Moroccan" today. When you see a recipe on a Spanish menu indicating its Moorish origin (*morunos*, *morisco*, or sometimes *árabe*), you can assume it will include spices like cumin, coriander, and cinnamon—flavors that became central to Iberian cuisine during the occupation and remained popular, even after the Moors were shown the door by Queen Isabela and King Ferdinand in 1492.

The first time I tasted *pinchos morunos*, a tasty skewer of marinated pork, I was in a tapas bar in Seville. My in-laws were watching our daughters, so my husband Lee and I had a few precious hours to wander around the city like "grown-ups." We followed our noses to a small bar in El Arenal, not far from the famous Giralda, and ordered a few items from the menu along with some local wine. I wish I could remember the name of the place. What I do remember is that the pork was succulent, the spices were intoxicating, and I was sitting at a table without being offered crayons. Heaven.

Traditionally, *pinchos morunos* are made from pork. I think of the choice as a small act of defiance from a country that was occupied by people who wouldn't touch the stuff for more than seven hundred years. Still, I don't think there's any need to keep the feud going, especially when chicken thighs make such a delightful version of the classic. I love to make these on a charcoal grill for an added punch of smokey flavor, but a gas grill or your broiler will also give you fantastic results.

While not as traditional, I absolutely love making veggie *pinchos*. You need sturdy vegetables that can stand up to marinating and skewering—I use mushrooms, red onion wedges, and tomatoes. Shishito peppers would be a fun choice, as would large zucchini or eggplant cubes. But whatever you do, don't be tempted to make pretty little individual kebabs combining the chicken and veggies! The ingredients have different cooking times. And, as my Uncle Neshan— shish kebab master extraordinaire—taught me, "No mixing skewers! The vegetables and meat can get together on your plate."

Serves: 4–6

Equipment you will need: Bamboo or metal skewers

Equipment that would be nice: a Microplane grater; a garlic press; a pastry brush; a charcoal grill; food prep gloves;

double-pointed skewers to keep round items from rolling on the grill; an instant-read thermometer

Ingredients:

1/3 c olive oil
Zest and juice of 2 large or 3 small lemons
1 1/2 t ground coriander
1 1/2 t ground cumin
1 t sweet or hot smoked paprika (I always use the *picante*)
2 t kosher salt, divided
2 t pepper, divided
3 cloves of garlic
2 lb boneless, skinless chicken thighs
10 oz cremini or baby bella mushrooms
4 plum tomatoes
2 red onions

1. Make the marinade: Add the oil, lemon zest, lemon juice, coriander, cumin, paprika, and 1 t each salt and pepper to a small bowl. Press the garlic and add to the bowl. (Alternatively, you can mince the garlic with a chef's knife, sprinkle it with a tiny bit of salt, and then run the sides of the knife over the garlic to smear it into a paste. Add to the bowl.) Whisk all the ingredients together. Divide the marinade between 2 1-gallon zip-top plastic bags (or reusable silicone bags, if you have them). Remove 1 T of marinade from one of the bags and put in a small prep bowl.
2. Trim any fat off the chicken thighs. Sprinkle the remaining salt and pepper over the meat. Cut each of the thighs into 4 pieces. Place the chicken pieces into the bag with

marinade, press the air out of the bag, and then seal. Gently massage the meat in the bag so that it's all coated with the marinade. Refrigerate for at least an hour, and up to 4 hours.

3. About 1 hour before you plan to cook, prepare the vegetables. Remove the stems from the mushroom caps. (These can be set aside to make mushroom stock or discarded). Add them to the other marinade bag.

4. Cut each of the tomatoes into 4 pieces and discard the seeds. Add to the mushrooms in the marinade bag. Press the air out of the marinade bag, then seal. Gently shake the bag so the vegetables are coated with marinade.

5. Peel the red onion. Cut in half through the stem ends, then cut in half again through the stem ends. Cut all four pieces in half at the equator. Keeping the onion layers intact, put all 8 pieces on a rimmed sheet pan. Lightly brush the pieces with the reserved marinade and cover with plastic wrap.

6. Fire up the charcoal or gas barbecue, if you're grilling. Make sure the grate is oiled before you set it over the coals. Otherwise, set your broiler to medium.

7. Line a platter with paper towels. Remove the chicken pieces from the marinade and lay them on the paper towels to remove excess marinade. Discard the remaining marinade. Repeat the process with the mushrooms and tomato pieces, separating them as you remove them from the bag.

8. Thread the chicken pieces onto the skewers. (Prep gloves make this job a bit neater, but they're not necessary.) Do not pack them tightly—you want as much surface area as possible exposed to cook the chicken evenly. Next, thread the mushrooms, tomatoes, and onions onto their own

skewers. Do your best to hold the onion layers together and discard any onion pieces too small for the skewer to go through.

9. If using a charcoal grill, arrange coals into an even layer so you can grill directly over them. With either grill, allow the grates to heat up, then place the skewers on them. (If your grill doesn't allow you to lay them all out at one time, grill in batches, starting with the chicken, then the onions, the mushrooms, and finally the tomatoes.)

10. Grill or broil the chicken until it's completely browned, with little flecks of charring toward the edges, about 4 or 5 minutes. Turn the skewers over and cook through, another 4 or 5 minutes. The chicken should be juicy, with no pink remaining. If using an instant-read thermometer, cook until the meat registers 160 degrees, being careful your thermometer isn't touching the skewers.

11. Grill the vegetables until they char and soften—the onions will take the longest time, then the mushrooms, and lastly the tomatoes.

12. I heap the chicken in the center of a large serving platter and surround it with the vegetables. But you can certainly serve the meat and vegetables separately if that's more your thing.

13. Serve with romesco sauce, if desired.

Romesco Sauce

———

Romesco sauce is a tomato-based, good-with-everything condiment from Catalunya. Making it is a bit like making a pesto or salsa verde, but it's made thick by the surprising addition of bread. Once it's in your fridge, you'll find yourself using it to add a little Iberian sunshine to any meal. I pair it with veggies (raw or cooked), eggs, and any grilled meat, including my *pinchos de pollo*. And it freezes well, so you can stash leftovers away and thaw it out to lend some homemade goodness to a busy day when all you have time for is grabbing a rotisserie chicken from the supermarket on the way home. At least, that's my strategy.

1/2 c + 2 T olive oil
1 small head garlic
3 plum tomatoes
1 c slivered almonds
12 oz jar roasted red peppers in olive oil, drained*
3 oz sturdy white bread, such as a pan basico, a baguette, or an Italian loaf
1–2 t smoked paprika
3 T sherry vinegar

Salt and pepper, to taste

Yield: about 1 1/2 c sauce

Equipment you will need: a food processor or blender; parchment paper; aluminum foil

1. Preheat the oven to 450 degrees.
2. First, roast the garlic. Cut a thin layer off the top of the garlic head so that a cross-section of the cloves is visible. Remove the outer layers of garlic skin, leaving enough to hold the head together. Place the head, root side down, in the center of a piece of parchment paper big enough to wrap the head entirely. Drizzle with 1 T olive oil and pull the corners up over the garlic head, then twist the excess paper around the top of the head. Place the parchment-wrapped head in the center of a sheet of aluminum foil and repeat the procedure to secure the parchment, making sure none of the head is exposed. Place the garlic in the middle of the oven and roast for about 40–50 minutes, until the cloves are soft and give easily when squeezed. Remove the garlic head from the oven and allow to cool for about 5 minutes, then carefully unwrap. Separate the cloves and press the bottom of each gently to "pop" them out of their skins. Place the roasted garlic cloves in the food processor or blender.
3. Roast the tomatoes. Line a small-rimmed baking sheet with parchment paper. Place the tomatoes on the pan and drizzle with 1 T olive oil. Rub the tomatoes to coat with the oil, then season them lightly with salt and pepper. Add to the oven and roast for about 20 minutes. Carefully turn the tomatoes over, then continue roasting until

they are soft, charred, and blistered in some places, about 25–30 minutes more. Remove the pan from the oven and set on a cooling rack. Allow to cool for about 5 minutes on a cooling rack and add the tomatoes and any accumulated juices to the food processor or blender.

4. While the tomatoes and garlic are roasting, add the almonds to a cool skillet. Set on a burner over low-medium heat. Stir frequently to make sure all sides are an equal golden brown, and you can smell a toasty, nutty aroma. Remove the pan from the heat and transfer the almonds to a plate. When the nuts are cool, add to the food processor or blender.

5. Dice the bread roughly (no need to be fancy here) and add it to the food processor, along with the drained pepper, smoked paprika, and sherry vinegar. Turn on the food processor, and while it is running, slowly add the olive oil through the feed tube until the mixture becomes a thick paste. Continue to process until the sauce is completely smooth, stopping and scraping down the sides if necessary.

6. Remove the sauce from the food processor to a bowl with a lid. Taste and adjust seasoning if necessary. Refrigerate until ready to use.

*Note: you can certainly roast your own red peppers and skin them for this recipe, but using the jarred variety makes getting this on the table a heck of a lot easier.

The "Spanish" Green Beans

———

As a toddler, my daughter Abbey would have happily lived on carbs and cheese alone. Most fruits were okay. She pretty much avoided meat if she could. And she definitely hated everything about green vegetables. Sure, every mom knows kids need to eat actual green things to thrive. But my daughter resisted green vegetables from the very first introduction, turning dinner into the exact kind of battle of wills that leaves all parties frustrated and exhausted. Her face scrunched up, she turned her head away, and she clamped her mouth shut, no matter how many times I tried to get her to "open the tunnel and let Thomas the Tank Engine in!" I tried every brand of baby food, even the crazy expensive organic stuff—no dice. I tried cooking the veggies myself and pureeing them—still no good.

This is why it totally got my attention on our first trip to Spain when my toddler ate an entire bowl of gazpacho, *including the sautéed green beans that were garnishing it.* No fussing.

No pleas to remove the offensive veggies from the premises. No pained expression. What was going on here? Despite the prevailing wisdom that babies and toddlers prefer bland food, it finally dawned on me that maybe green vegetables needed more flavor, not less, to pass my toddler's taste test.

When I got back to the US, I decided to test my theory. I came up with a dish of green beans in a sauce that had the predominant flavors of the gazpacho she'd liked so much—sweet tomatoes, warm paprika, zingy sherry vinegar—and presented it to Abigail with a flourish. It's fair to say she looked dubious. But when I chirpily explained that these were just like the green beans she LOVED in Spain, she picked one up. She sniffed it. And she finally put it into her mouth. She chewed. She swallowed. And she picked up another bean. Success! Seriously, I felt like I'd won a James Beard Award because a toddler willingly ate a vegetable.

No surprise, green beans with a gazpacho-inspired tomato sauce became part of our weekly diet. The recipe got tweaked some over the years, sometimes even including bits of Serrano ham to make it a bit fancier. But it has remained a family favorite. Somehow, on weekly menus and in discussions, the dish became known as "The Spanish Green Beans." And since they were, in fact, inspired by the glorious cuisine of that country, I feel like it's okay to keep "Spanish" in the title. Just know that if they're not a big hit with your book club or family—and I really don't think that's going to happen, considering how many of my friends and family have now approved this dish—you can put it all on me. And Abbey's strange toddler palate.

Yield: 4 servings (easily doubled)

Equipment you will need: a vegetable steamer; a sauté pan or Dutch oven with a lid

Ingredients:

8 ounces thin green beans (haricot vert)
1 yellow onion
3 cloves garlic
2 T extra virgin olive oil, divided (it's a big part of the flavor, so if you have a nice Spanish one, this is the time to break it out)
1 t smoked paprika
1 14-oz can diced tomatoes
1/2 c water
2 t sherry vinegar
Salt and pepper, to taste

1. Trim the stem ends off the green beans. Put about 2 inches of water in a lidded pot large enough to accommodate your vegetable steaming basket and bring it to a boil. Place the steamer basket in the pot, place the green beans on top of the basket, and cover the pot with a tight-fitting lid. Reduce the heat to low, just enough to keep the water at a heavy simmer.
2. Steam the beans for about 5 minutes, until they are tender but still firm. Remove the beans from the steamer and place in a medium bowl. Set aside.
3. Finely dice the onion and the garlic. Place one tablespoon of the oil in a sauté pan over medium heat. When the oil begins to shimmer, add the onion to the pan, and

sauté gently, stirring frequently, until the onion is soft and golden, about 5–7 minutes.

4. Add the garlic to the pan and continue to sauté until the garlic becomes fragrant, but not brown, about 2 minutes more.

5. Add the smoked paprika to the pan, and sauté one minute more.

6. Add the diced tomatoes and their juices and the water to the pan. Bring to a boil, then reduce the heat to a simmer. Cover and cook for about 15–20 minutes, stirring occasionally, until the tomatoes begin to break down and form a sauce. (You may need to add a bit more water, one tablespoon at a time, if the sauce gets too dry.)

7. Add salt and pepper to the sauce to taste. Then carefully add the steamed green beans and the vinegar to sauce in the pan. Stir to coat the beans in the sauce. Cover and simmer for about 2 minutes, until the green beans are warmed through.

8. Test one last time for salt. Place the beans and sauce in a serving dish, then drizzle with the remaining tablespoon of olive oil.

9. Serve immediately or cover and serve at room temperature.

Arroz con Leche

———

Comfort food is people food. And by that, I mean it's the memory of the people with whom I shared the food that brings me comfort. This is why I can never think about rice pudding (that's English for arroz con leche) without thinking of my Aunt Marion. She absolutely loved it. And one college summer, while I was staying in Queens while working in the city, I was at Aunt Marion's apartment for dinner, and we then decided we needed dessert. Now my aunt was an excellent baker, but this was a stinking hot, after-work kind of thing, and we weren't up for starting a big project. But there was some rice in the house, sugar, cinnamon, and some milk. We didn't have a recipe in those way-back days before the internet. But we both knew how to make rice. How hard could it be?

Hard was right. As in, the rice came out totally hard. We both tasted it, made a face, and decided the better part of valor was putting it in the garbage and going out for ice cream. The "comforting" part is that my aunt and I laughed about that ridiculous rice pudding attempt for years after. It was an inside joke that never got old. So, it was my Aunt Marion

I was thinking of when I decided that arroz con leche would be a great addition to this menu. And I was determined to make one that she would have loved.

Arroz con leche—literally "rice with milk" in Spanish—is a quintessential Spanish dessert. You'll often see it, along with flan, ice cream, and a slice of fruit tart, as a dessert choice on the "Menu del Dia," a three-course prix fixe lunch available at restaurants all over Spain. At its best, it's a bowl of creamy, cinnamon-ey goodness. It's amazing served warm, especially in the colder months, but it's also really nice chilled in the warm months. And like any recipe that's in the DNA of a culture, everyone has their own version of it.

The classic rice used in Spain is called "bomba," a type of short-grained rice known for its starring role in *paella*. But it can be difficult to find in the US—and it's quite expensive when you order it online. So, I turned to another famous—and widely available—European short-grained rice: arborio. By soaking it before cooking, I was able to somewhat reduce the starch and soften it up a bit before cooking. I used creamy dairy to give it a decadent feel—but almond milk would make a fine substitute. Cinnamon is the classic seasoning, and I didn't see any reason to mess with that. But I wanted it to taste particularly Spanish. Thinking back to a spring trip to Cordoba, where the smell of the oranges that grow on every street was so strong that I thought, "This must be where potpourri was invented," I added a healthy shot of orange peel to the finished dessert. The result is familiar, yet still a little special—perfect with a cup of coffee or a glass of red wine.

Yield: 8 1/2 c servings

Equipment you will need: a fine mesh strainer; a heavy-bottomed saucepan or Dutch oven

Equipment that would be nice: a Microplane grater

Ingredients:

1 c arborio rice
1 c heavy whipping cream
3–4 c whole or 2 percent milk
1/2 c sugar
1/2 t salt
2 cinnamon sticks (or 1/2 t ground cinnamon)
1 unwaxed orange
Whipped cream, for serving (optional)

1. Place the arborio rice in a medium bowl. Cover with cool water and allow to sit for 15 minutes. Drain over the sink into a fine mesh strainer. Return the rice to the bowl, cover with water, and allow to sit for another 15 minutes. Strain the rice completely.
2. Set a heavy-bottomed saucepan over medium heat. Add the cream, 3 cups of milk the sugar, salt, and cinnamon sticks to the pot. Add the drained rice and stir until the mixture is at a heavy simmer, then reduce the heat to low.
3. Simmer the milk mixture, stirring often to make sure no rice sticks to the bottom of the pan, until the rice is cooked all the way through but not mushy. This can take between 35 and 50 minutes. But there's no rushing it. Low and slow is the way to go here.

4. When almost all the liquid has been absorbed—a rubber spatula pulled along the bottom of the pan leaves a clean track behind it for a moment—taste the rice. If it's at all al dente (fine for risotto, but not what we're after), warm 1/4 c milk in the microwave, and stir it into the arroz con leche. Allow to cook for another 5 minutes or so. Continue the process until the rice is cooked through and bathed in a creamy sauce—you do not want it to be dry because it's going to set.

5. Using a peeler or a Microplane grater, zest the orange, making sure to avoid any of the white pith. If using a peeler, mince the orange peel.

6. When the rice is completely cooked, remove from the heat. Remove the cinnamon sticks and discard. Stir 2 t orange zest into the arroz con leche.

7. Distribute into 8 half-cup dessert cups, ramekins, or tea cups. Cover the pudding with plastic wrap, pressing it down so a skin doesn't form on the top.

8. When the desserts come to room temperature, place them in the refrigerator until ready to serve.

9. When ready to serve, remove the plastic wrap. Top with whipped cream and a bit of orange zest, if desired.

Taking Book Club to the Next Level: Pepita Jiménez

BEVERAGES TO OFFER:

Non-alcoholic drinks: The only non-alcoholic beverage referred to in *Pepita Jiménez* is coffee, and hot or iced coffee would be a perfect accompaniment to this book club buffet. But even richer and more delicious would be *chocolate caliente*, or hot chocolate. The Spanish version of the drink is based on dark chocolate melted in whole milk, sweetened to taste, then thickened with cornstarch—the better to adhere to those delectable *churros* at breakfast time. It's pretty much a confection but would certainly pair well with the *arroz con leche* in this chapter.

Alcoholic drinks: Wine serves an important role in the novel, as Don Luis describes the operations of his father's farm to his uncle the Dean: "visiting the wine-vaults and cask stores, superintending the clarifying, rebottling, and perfecting of the wines . . . [meeting] with dealers from Xeres who come to buy our wine in order to convert it into sherry, are here the daily occupation of the gentry." So, you can't go wrong serving sherry or any red or white Spanish wine, or even Spain's contribution to sparkling wines, cava, on their own. But sangria, a punch of wine, sparkling water, fruit, or fruit juices, would be just as authentic and is perfect for a book club brunch.

MUSIC TO PLAY/VIDEOS TO STREAM:

The music of guitars and castanets is referenced throughout *Pepita Jiménez*. Searching streaming services such as Spotify, Pandora, and Amazon Music for "traditional Spanish guitar music" yields dozens of playlists and albums to choose from, creating the perfect soundtrack for your book club meeting. Even more on point, you might wish to play Albeniz's beautiful opera of the same name and listen to the sweet soprano of Pepita as she falls in love with Don Luis' tenor. The original libretto was in English, but it has been translated into both Italian and French. Multiple cast albums are available through streaming services, and individual arias appear at various internet locations, including YouTube.

WHAT TO BRING/TABLESCAPES:

Where you see an olive bar, I see Tapas! Seriously, anyone who doesn't want to cook can make a meaningful contribution to a Pepita Jiménez book club by bringing containers of olives, peppers, and artichokes along to the event—no Spanish gathering would happen without them. Also readily available are Spanish cheeses and the king of Spanish hams, serrano. A charcuterie board including those, along with grapes and olives, would be a simple and delicious addition to book club. A Spanish table would likely have a colorful tablecloth and napkins, so break out your prettiest florals for the occasion. And if you're meeting in summer, a fan next to each place setting would be a thoughtful addition—Spanish women still routinely pull them out of their bags to create a pleasant breeze when out in the midday sun.

On Cranky Toddlers and the Kindness of Strangers in Barcelona

---

My husband and I love to travel, and we decided early in our marriage that any children we had were coming along for the ride. Our oldest, Abigail, was such a seasoned traveler that as a three-year-old, she told an airline attendant she was going to need to "gate check my stroller."

Abbey's first trip to Europe was to visit her grandparents, who were living for a year in Barcelona when Abbey was two. We thought we had planned the trip with about the precision with which Eisenhower planned the Normandy campaign. We booked our overnight flight through Brussels, thinking we would have plenty of time in the airport to pick up a better-than-decent breakfast before our connecting flight.

Rookie parenting mistake.

Our flight from New York was delayed multiple times, our departure time creeping past Abigail's dinner time and then her bedtime. After midnight, we finally fell into our seats. But when we got off the ground, we found out that our normally sound-sleeping toddler was awakened by every pass of the drink cart down the aisle. She finally slept, but I never did. So, we were a pretty bedraggled bunch when we bolted off the plane in Brussels, running frantically through the Brussels airport with a toddler, her stroller, her diaper bag, and all the other things we'd devised to amuse her on the long trip. We just made the Barcelona flight—but we had to give up the tasty croissant, coffee, and chocolate we had planned for our Belgian layover.

We had some provisions in the diaper bag, of course—the ubiquitous Goldfish, some applesauce, enough juice boxes, and Parmalat milks to stave off dehydration. But we'd kept the food to a minimum, knowing that bringing food items into Europe can be problematic. We were exhausted and hungry when we finally got out of the cab in the Barcelona suburb of San Cugat and wearily greeted my in-laws, looking forward to getting our jet-lagged daughter something to eat and a long nap.

But then we realized we had another problem: since they had no way of leaving us a key, my in-laws had been waiting around for us to arrive before they went shopping. So, there we were, on a street in Catalunya with a cranky toddler and little food in the house—and we had arrived at the dreaded "no food zone" time between lunch and dinner.

Let me explain: needing a meal at 3 p.m. in Spain is a problem. Since it was my first trip to Spain myself, I had no idea how big of a problem it would actually be. In Barcelona in the nineties, there wasn't a fast food option on every corner (frankly, to the Catalan's credit, there still isn't). Food professionals had stringent schedules, and when the kitchen was closed after lunch, it was literally *closed*: nothing was served until it opened again for dinner. Many bars, however, remained open for customers looking for a place to linger over a libation and chat, often along with some ready-made tapas. But a full meal at three o'clock in the afternoon? Not likely.

We examined our choices. Starting a trip to the grocery store to gather ingredients for even a simple meal seemed a daunting task in light of Abbey's irritable state, which was deteriorating by the moment. So, in desperation, my father-in-law, Pat, ran over to the closest small bar/restaurant to their apartment. In this place, he and my mother-in-law often made a meal of the *Menú del Día*, a prix fixe lunch that included an appetizer, main course, and a glass of local wine. It was a tiny place, not much wider than a hallway, with a small bar on the left and tables crammed along the right side. The bar owner walked out and greeted my father-in-law, and my father-in-law explained what was going on.

My Spanish was pretty rusty from lack of use, but the conversation seemed to go on a long time, sprinkled with some words I could understand: "baby," "hungry," "New Yorkers," and, I'm pretty sure, "disaster"—I hoped that was referring to the airline, and not his daughter-in-law. Standing on that corner, hungry and defeated, I felt like the vacation we'd looked forward to for so long was already a disaster. I wanted to cry, but Abbey was already doing that. Then, finally, looking down the street at our wilted crew, the owner took pity on us.

The bar owner rolled up his sleeves and cooked what I still remember as the most delicious *lomo a la plancha*, a well-seasoned pork cutlet pounded very thin and then cooked on a hot griddle with hot irons on top to keep the pork from curling. It was perfectly brown and so tender that a knife was unnecessary. The pork was served with a side of French fries, crispy and golden on the outside, fluffy on the inside. Abbey would have been happy with just the fries. But instead, the owner called up to his apartment and had his wife bring down some soup she had made for their own lunch. Shiny black beans arrived floating in a broth redolent with smoky *pimentón*. Abbey sat quietly as the bowl was placed in front of her, grabbed a spoon, and dug in.

The simple meal turned the tide. And our once-cranky toddler, now full and getting her second wind, turned on the charm. In preparation for the trip, we had taught Abigail to say "please" and "thank you" in Catalan (not Spanish, because most Barcelonans speak Catalan as their first language) on the recommendation of my in-laws. Abbey, a born performer, stood on her chair and thanked the woman for the soup with a sing-song, "Moltes gràcies." The owners' reaction was priceless: they were thrilled. I think they were almost as thankful that we had thought to do that small thing to honor their unique culture as we were for the fine meal. They asked about her for years afterward whenever my in-laws went to the bar; they even sent her a little gift when they heard she had made her first holy communion. Such a long-lasting connection over such a simple meal, graciously shared.

MARRIAGE AND ROMANCE IN KING ARTHUR'S COURT

Photo credit: Lee Ahern

The Book Recommendation: Erec and Enide

It's a romance, but the couple is married for most of it. The man doesn't want any help, but the woman keeps saving his life because she's actually paying attention. From the outside, the relationship appears a bit dysfunctional, but ultimately they hang in there and support each other. *Erec and Enide* was written by Chrétien de Troyes in the year 1170. It's one of the oldest of the Arthurian tales, and as a woman who's been married for nearly thirty years, I couldn't help thinking that very little has changed in close to a thousand years of marriage. Any person who's ever been in a long-term relationship can put herself in Enide's dainty shoes.

Erec et Enide was the first of five Arthurian extant epic poems by Chrétien de Troyes. Because they were written for performance (and not for quiet, individual reflection, as we so often interact with poetry now), the poems are plot-driven and full of magical characters, mysterious events, and a lot of blood-thirsty combat. But the story also offers a rare insight into medieval marriage, or at least Chrétien de Troyes' understanding of it. While the wedding is typically the place where most romantic works conclude, Erec and Enide's nuptials take place early in the poem. What we experience for the rest of the story is the titular characters trying to make their medieval marriage work. And that's what makes *Erec and Enide* such an interesting choice for a book club read.

When we first encounter Erec, a king's son, he is the second most powerful knight in King Arthur's court, assigned to protect Queen Guinevere. When the Queen's entourage is insulted by a powerful knight, his accompanying dwarf (dwarves often signal evil in medieval literature, an upsetting feature of the genre), and a beautiful young woman, an armor-less Erec gives chase. He follows them to a town in which the evil knight, Yder, will compete in a tournament to win a hawk for his fair companion. Erec finds a place to stay with a noble family that has fallen on hard times. When he meets Enide, the daughter of the family, he is overwhelmed by her beauty, despite the fact that she is dressed in rags. He borrows some armor, vanquishes the hometown favorite, and wins the hawk for Enide – along with her hand in marriage.

Confusingly, Erec will not allow Enide's cousin to give her decent clothes for the trip back to King Arthur's court, preferring to have the Queen clothe her instead. The reason for this is unclear in the text, but it may indicate that nothing found outside of the court would measure up to her beauty. Once she is properly adorned, Erec and Enide wed. Their wedding is followed by a surprisingly frank discussion of their wedding night—a discussion that would have scandalized any Regency reader. Erec wins a tournament, solidifying his place as one of the King's most powerful knights. And right then, seemingly at the top of his jousting game, he decides to leave the court and settle down into a life of peaceful domesticity.

Unfortunately, wedded bliss does not last long. Enide finds that Erec has become an object of ridicule since he no longer engages in chivalric pursuits, preferring only the company of his beautiful wife. Rather than revel in her position at the center of his life, Enide confronts him. It's a fascinating but jarring scene for the modern reader. While in the twenty-first century we're accustomed to the trope emanating from the protagonist having to choose between one's lover and one's friends, this medieval wife apparently sides with Erec's *cronies*, which forces us to consider the purpose of marriage in Chrétien's time. It seems that Enide feels her own position is diminished and even imperiled by Erec's withdrawal from courtly life. Deciding the honeymoon is clearly over, Erec tells Enide to pack her bags and follow him—apparently on a quest to recover his lost manhood. However, while Erec refuses to be parted from his wife, taking her along on chivalric travels, he admonishes her not to speak to him.

From there, the poem proceeds like other medieval romances, from test to test, with both Erec and Enide in and out of danger. Yet through it all, their devotion to each other is clear. Despite all admonitions, Enide warns Erec when she senses danger. Erec gets angry but acts on her information to save them anyway. It's clear the couple only survives by her disobeying him. So, at the critical moment when all is about to be lost, the reader is captivated, wondering if Enide will finally heed his command and be silent and thus condemn them both.

I love recommending *Erec and Enide* to book clubs because it's a quick read that opens so many avenues for discussion. What is behind Erec's shame, and what does that say about the hierarchy of relationships in medieval Europe compared with modern society? Why are words and names so crucial in the story, and what does it mean to share them – or take them away? How would Chrétien define a successful marriage, and do Erec and Enide ever achieve it? And, ultimately, how did the common understanding of a medieval romance come to include knights in shining armor saving damsels in distress when the oldest example of the genre defies the stereotype? That discussion alone would make for a memorable book club!

The World of Erec and Enide

———

Although Chrétien de Troyes's poems are based on the legends of King Arthur, who supposedly reigned in the West of Britain during the fifth century CE, *Erec and Enide*, as well as the rest of his Arthurian cycle, were written during the second half of the twelfth century. Since historical accuracy was not a hallmark of medieval art (witness the many paintings portraying biblical figures in medieval dress), the author's fictional accounts were likely more reflective of conditions in contemporary society than in early post-Roman Briton. Some of the major societal and artistic influences finding expression in Chrétien's works would have been feudalism, the Catholic Church, and the heightened status of women in the High Middle Ages.

The fact that stories about the court of a mythical king from western Britain came to define the genre of medieval romances in what is now southern France tells us a lot about both politics and communications during the medieval era.

Regarding politics, when the Roman Empire collapsed in the West at the end of the fifth century, it opened the way for a series of westward migrations by tribal peoples from what is now Germany and Eastern Europe. One of those groups, the Franks, gave its name to modern France. For a time, large-scale government was abandoned in favor of smaller fiefdoms that were defensible by local strongmen. These fiefdoms gradually coalesced into larger kingdoms, including the Holy Roman Empire, in addition to most of modern-day France, Belgium, the Netherlands, Germany, and Northern Italy. But borders and loyalties were fluid throughout the time period (500-1400 CE). Considering the importance of building alliances for mutual protection, powerful families used marriage as a way to solidify relationships. So a relatively small number of powerful families eventually crisscrossed Western Europe with marriage bonds. So this elite (though, eventually noble) class shared a more similar culture based on education, religion, and philosophical beliefs than geography might indicate.

One figure of particular importance in the development of medieval romances is Eleanor of Aquitaine, who inherited the Duchy of Aquitaine in her own right as the Poitiers heir, making her one of the richest and most powerful women in the world. She became Queen of France through her marriage to Louis VII in 1154 and participated in the Second Crusade to the Holy Land. Because her marriage to Louis VII failed to produce any male offspring, she was able to convince the Pope to grant her an annulment. After the annulment, she quickly married Henry II of England (was it truly a failed crusade then, for Eleanor). Although the English crown had held properties on the European mainland since the

Norman conquest in 1066, Eleanor extended the ties between Britain and the continent, especially as a patroness of the arts. Her daughter with Louis—Marie of France, Countess of Champagne—continued the Poitier family tradition of supporting scholars and artists, and Chrétien de Troyes was one of the artists she supported. Chrétien thanks her specifically for her contribution to one of his later romances, *Lancelot, The Knight of the Cart*.

The Catholic Church provided the unifying framework for medieval Europe. According to Thomas Cahill, author of *How the Irish Saved Civilization: The Untold Story of Ireland's Heroic Role from the Fall of Rome to the Rise of Medieval Europe*, monasteries were repositories for both sacred and historical texts. With confrontations between indigenous and migratory peoples often ending in military conflict, the monasteries' remote locations served to preserve most of what was left in Western Europe from the times of the Roman occupations. The monks did far more than copy and distribute biblical texts. Many became authors in their own right, codifying local legends and oral history on parchment.

As territorial lines became redrawn and life became more peaceful and less difficult, the Church, through the monasteries, became a source of education and scholarship. The Church took a primary role in education, establishing in the period the great universities of Bologna, Paris, Oxford, Cambridge, Salamanca, and Montpellier during the period, through which the stored cultural knowledge of the Church was shared. This is one likely route for the transfer of Arthurian legends into the courts of southern France.

In addition to its focus on education, high medieval Christianity was characterized by an increasing devotion to the Blessed Virgin Mary, the mother of Jesus Christ, today known as "The Cult of the Virgin." Many scholars have attempted to explain the phenomenon, including the historical relationship between agrarian societies and female deities, alongside holdover sentiment from the Greco-Roman Cult of Isis. But whatever the origins, dedication to Mary during the era can be seen in the many cathedrals and churches sanctified to her, as well as her many titles.

At about the same time, we see a shift in the status of elite women in the literature, focused on the concept of "courtly love." Since marriages at all levels of society were commonly arranged for the benefit of families, women were generally considered a form of property to be transferred, either for money (as in a bride price or dowry) or for other contractual accommodations, during the early medieval period. Marital love as described in *Erec and Enide* would have been exceedingly rare, especially among elites—and indeed, it is Erec's unrestrained desire for Enide that precipitates the main crisis in the poem. However, the literary device of "courtly love," in which a knight's fealty to one's lord is transferred to an unfulfilled desire for and obeisance to the lord's lady, shifts literary power to women in medieval romances. We see this kind of relationship in the way the love between the Knights of the Round Table and Queen Guinevere is described throughout the Arthurian cycle. For example, note the description of Erec's homecoming with Enide:

"They saw Erec now approaching,

And the lady he was bringing

From afar they recognized him

At the instant they first saw him.

Guinevere was filled with joy;

All the court, without alloy,

Were joyful at his coming there,

For all loved him in equal share."

Academics disagree about whether the Cult of the Virgin and the rise of the concept of courtly love are related, although Dante certainly conflates them in the character of Beatrice in his *Divine Comedy* later in the medieval period. Academics also disagree (because that's what they do) about whether the literary device of courtly love transferred to society at all, although most social historians don't believe there was any impact among the lower classes. It is possible that what is actually being expressed through courtly love is the appreciation for the patronage of powerful women such as Eleanor of Aquitaine and her daughter Marie of France. But, as we also know, life imitates art—in this period, courtship rituals were established, with women figuring more prominently as actors (though rarely solo) rather than mere objects, both in society and within Western literature.

Essentials of Medieval French Cuisine

——

Since medieval Europe came immediately after Roman Empire Europe, the people were already familiar with foodstuffs from Asia, Africa, and the Middle East that had flowed into Western Europe through Latin trade routes. Some of these crops transplanted easily and remained part of European cuisine from Roman times onward; apples, apricots, dates, dill, and chickpeas are just a few examples. By necessity, most medieval cooks were locavores, making the most of whatever was fresh at the moment and preserving what was abundant for leaner times. But in addition to availability, the medieval diet was shaped by two powerful external forces: the ancient concept of the humors and the liturgical calendar.

THE HUMORS

Reaching all the way back to the Greek physician Galen, humoral theory says that human health is aligned with the four elements (earth, water, air, and fire), represented in the human body by the four humors (black bile, phlegm, blood, and yellow bile (choler)). The humors were characterized by a combination of heat and humidity. Black bile was cold and dry, like earth. Phlegm was cold and moist like water. Blood was hot and moist, like air. And choler was hot and dry, like fire. If all the humors were in proper balance, the human body would be happy and healthy. If they were out of balance, sickness was the result. Belief in the humors guided health practice for nearly two millennia.

According to Karen Lyon, writing for Folger Library's *Shakespeare and Beyond* blog, the dominant humor in people's bodies controlled their temperament: "Sanguine people were thought to be ruddy and cheerful, phlegmatics pale and listless, cholerics jaundiced and angry, and melancholics dark and sad (but often creative)." So, in an effort to achieve a balance between the humors, medieval dietary wisdom prescribed eating the foods *opposite* the patient's dominant characteristic. Thus, sanguine people were told to eat foods characterized as cold and dry, such as vinegar and other sour foods (not that it makes much sense to call vinegar, which is clearly a liquid, dry, but it also doesn't make much sense to try and eat your way to being *less* cheerful). Melancholic personalities were prescribed sweet foods, which were characterized as hot and wet—it's hard not to think about how often we still turn to sweets when we're sad, isn't it? Phlegmatic temperaments were thought to be improved by bitter and salty foods, which were characterized as hot and dry. And choleric temperaments were soothed by cold, moist foods, which were mostly bland and lean, which would have made plenty of sense if it was a stomach ailment affecting someone's disposition.

From an early time, it's clear that people noted the link between food and both physical and mental health. In the wake of the Scientific Revolution, it's easy to dismiss medieval belief in the humors as "quaint" or "silly." But the urge to find the right food to cure all our problems certainly remains, as the sheer quantities of kale and acai berries regularly consumed in smoothies nowadays indeed attests.

THE CHURCH CALENDAR

The Roman Catholic liturgical calendar guided the medieval diet as much as the seasons did. According to food and book blogger Rebecca Selman, the Church labeled nearly a third of the year as "fast days," when no meat could be eaten. Fasts were declared weekly on Wednesday, Friday, and Saturday, as well during the seasons of Advent, preceding Christmas, and Lent, preceding Easter. Fasting was strict, prohibiting all meat and animal-derived products, including eggs and dairy products. This explains the many references to almond milk in medieval recipes.

The liturgical calendar also included twelve Ember days (a Wednesday, Friday, and Saturday during one week in each season) set aside for prayers of thanksgiving for nature's abundance. On those days, people fasted from meat, but eggs and dairy could be included in meals. There are a number of recipes for "Ember Day Tarts" in historical recipe collections. Constance B. Hieatt, Brenda Hosington, and Sharon Butler, authors of *Pleyn Delit: Medieval Cookery for Modern Cooks*, include a recipe from "The Forme of Curye" that includes onions, herbs, cheese, eggs, and spices baked in a tart shell, which bears an incredible likeness to the modern-day quiche.

Of course, feast days were for celebration, and many of the extant medieval recipes derive from them. Catholic Culture, an encyclopedic website dedicated to all things Catholic, lists dozens of recipes for foods associated with Catholic feast days, from stollen at Christmas to babka at Easter and soul cakes for All Saints Day. The sweetness and richness of those feast day foods must have been a real treat after the many fast days of the period.

BREAD AND WINE

In her exhaustive food history of France, *Savoir-Faire*, Mary-ann Trebban traces the foundations of French gastronomy to the Middle Ages. Unsurprising, in a country whose eating was dominated by the Catholic Church, the two food items included in the sacrifice of the Mass—namely, bread and wine—became staples of life. While we might be inclined to think of white bread as a relatively recent addition to the French diet, refined white flour was used for *pain blanc* during the Middle Ages. Its shape has changed, however. In the medieval era, bread was baked in the round, not long like the classic baguette, probably to symbolize the host offered at mass. The many fast days associated with the liturgical calendar made bread critical to the medieval diet, as it was likely to be the primary source of calories fueling the populace on any given day.

The rise of wine production in France was similarly tied to the Catholic Church. The number of monastic communities, which devoted themselves to lives of contemplation and prayer, grew throughout the medieval era. The monasteries supported the Church, and since bread and wine were necessary for the mass, monks cultivated both wheat and grapes, in addition to all the vegetables and herbs necessary to sustain them and the laypeople associated with them within their gardens. The cultivation of vineyards formed part of the monks' devotional practice, and their focus led to both innovations and specializations, depending on the part of the region in which they were located. The dominant grapes and wine-making techniques throughout France today grew out of the abbeys and monasteries that controlled wine production in France throughout the medieval era. Extant medieval recipes make liberal use of wine and wine products, such as verjus, so it's clear that wine was available to most members of the population, not just the clerics.

USE OF SPICES

Let's start with what is not true: There is no evidence that medieval cooks used spices to cover the taste of spoiled food. They seem to have been well aware of the effect of time on their foodstuffs, and the number of extant recipes devoted to preservation indicates that the practice was extensive. However, recipes include references to several "powders," or spice blends, with powdered ginger, nutmeg, cinnamon, sugar, and pepper routinely included. Despite its expense, Saffron was also a popular spice, with its entry into the territory now known as France facilitated by its proximity to Moor-controlled Iberia. Similar spice blends show up in both sweet and spicy dishes from the period, which indicates their widespread popularity.

ERIC AND ENIDE: RECIPES FOR BOOK CLUB

That night they partook of every
Single thing the heart would wish.

Fowl and venison, fruit and fish,
And wines in all their variety.

But better still was the company!

Asparagus with a Savory Egg Sauce

———

I had a childhood friend whose English family referred to "asparagus" as "a spear of grass." This always seemed weird to me, seeing as the asparagus at my house was sort of gray and mushy and came out of a can. The vegetables and accompanying green liquid were dumped into a small saucepan and heated to a boil—the contents of which were then plopped into a cereal bowl and topped with a pat of butter. It was more "string" than "spear," and to say the Connolly kids were not big fans is a wild understatement.

But once I started going to nice restaurants, I found a whole new appreciation for my former vegetable nemesis, and it slowly became a mainstay of my vegetable repertoire. I learned to steam it so that it was tender-crisp and presented a vivid green. I sauced it with lemony vinaigrettes, creamy Green Goddess dressing, and rich butter sauces. I roasted it. I barbecued it. I added it to various types of pasta and risottos.

But nothing prepared me for the near euphoria with which asparagus is greeted each spring in Germany. While teaching in Germany one spring, I learned that *Spargelzeit,* or "Asparagus Season," runs from mid-April to June 24, St. John's Day on the Catholic liturgical calendar. During that short window, tables in grocery stores and farmer's markets groan under the weight of the white stalks preferred by locals. Roadside stands offer *Frische Spargel* along the Romantic Road. Food magazines showcase new and exciting recipes featuring Germany's vegetable darling. Every menu includes an asparagus special. And then, just when you think you never want to eat another *spargel* anything, it's over. Gone. No longer in the stores. The *spargel*-obsessed move on to the next seasonal offering—cherries—and don't look back.

For an American used to having year-round access to almost any vegetable through the wonder of imported produce, the quick change was a bit of a shock. But that seasonal, local eating is probably very close to the way Europeans have always dined: eat what's fresh, preserve what you can't eat, and then focus on the next crop to be harvested. So, if you really want an authentic medieval experience, make this recipe in the springtime, when asparagus of all colors arrive at your local farmer's market. But if you're reading *Erec and Enide* in autumn, it will be almost as delicious with super-thin asparagus from a hothouse.

Serves: 4–6

Equipment you will need: a blender or a food processor; a vegetable peeler

Ingredients:

1 lb asparagus spears, any color
1/2 c white wine
1/2 c unsweetened chicken stock or vegetable stock
1 hard-boiled egg, peeled
2 green onions, whites only
1/8 t ground ginger
1/8 t ground cinnamon
1 t vinegar
1/4 cup parsley
Salt and pepper to taste

1. Trim the woody ends from the asparagus by holding them on the woody end and just below the flowery top and bending. The asparagus should snap where the tender part of the stalk begins. Set the woody ends aside.
2. Half-fill a pan large enough to hold all the asparagus at once with water. Bring the water to a boil and add 1–2 tablespoons of salt. Add the asparagus tops to the pan and reduce heat to simmer. Cook for about 2–5 minutes, depending on the size of your asparagus spears, until the stalks are bright green and easily pierced with a knife. Drain in a colander and rinse with cold water to stop cooking and preserve color. Set the asparagus on a serving platter.
3. Peel the woody ends of the asparagus with a vegetable peeler and then trim the very end of the stalk and discard. Chop the remaining woody ends roughly. Add the wine, stock, and woody asparagus ends to a small saucepan and bring to a boil. Reduce to a simmer, cover the pan and cook for five minutes. Remove from heat. Remove

the asparagus ends from the liquid and discard them. Reserve the liquid.

4. Add the broth and wine mixture to a blender. Roughly chop the green onions and egg and add to the blender along with the spices. Puree until quite smooth, then return the mixture to the saucepan over medium-high heat, stirring constantly, until the liquid is reduced by half. You will have a thin, viscous sauce.

5. Remove from heat. Stir in vinegar and parsley. Taste for salt and pepper.

Pork and Veggie Hand Pies

Until my first trip to Europe, every savory pie I had eaten came directly from the freezer section of the local King Kullen supermarket. My grandmother, Mary Ellen Connolly, grew up in Hell's Kitchen, then a rough neighborhood in Manhattan. She lived in apartments with cooktops, though rarely had an oven. So, while Grandma could look into a seemingly empty refrigerator and whip up a fantastic stew, she was decidedly not a baker. She did love to eat baked things, however. So, whenever she babysat for us, one of the dinner staples was Swanson's Frozen Chicken Pot Pie. My mom would make sure the freezer was stocked with them because it was almost no work for Grandma, and it was something all of us would eat. For reasons I can no longer understand, I absolutely loved the job of using the paring knife to cut the vents in the frozen pie dough. We just popped them in the oven, and an hour later, dinner was on the table. The crust was often burnt, as it took so long for the frozen filling to cook. But somehow, it was a special treat.

Fast forward to my time living above a pub as an exchange student, and I found out that savory pies came in all shapes and flavors. I had my first Cornish pasty on the street of Windsor. The sign called it a "walking pie," which made sense since tourists walked around with them as they waited on the humongous queue leading to Windsor Castle. A big wedge often served as dinner upstairs, as well as in the pub downstairs.

Pies have a long history in Europe. According to BBC Bitesize, they were a staple of the medieval kitchen because the thick pie shell preserved the (mostly savory) contents hidden beneath. But I imagine that from a culinary standpoint, it also had something to do with the pie shell helping prevent the uneven heat from medieval fires reaching the precious contents inside and drying them out. At some point in the Middle Ages, pies became part of the entertainment at banquets, with chefs playing a game of one-upmanship that included baking actual, real-life entertainers into the pie— sort of a precursor to Debbie Reynolds in *Singin' in the Rain*, but involving an actual oven.

According to *Pie: A Global History* by Janet Clarkson, medieval pie crusts were not eaten by the wealthy—they acted more like disposable Dutch ovens. She posits that the gravy-soaked crust probably wasn't wasted and was most likely divvied up by the house staff. The hand pie dough recipe I've given you (pg 213) is rich and sturdy, though definitely meant to be eaten when filled with this savory, sweet, and sour filling. The pork filling gets its sweetness from raisins and rutabagas; and its sourness from a wine reduction. The pies get their distinctive "medieval" aroma from a combination of ginger and cinnamon, but considering the popularity of Southeast Asian cuisines that heavily utilize the same spices, I think the combination will be right at home at any modern book club meeting.

Equipment you will need: a colander; a rolling pin

Equipment that would be nice: a bird's nest strainer; a pastry brush; an instant-read thermometer

Ingredients:

3 leeks—whites and light green parts only
1 rutabaga or 3 turnips (about 1–1 1/2 lb)
2 T salt, divided
3 T olive oil
1 lb ground pork
2 carrots, peeled and finely chopped
1 1/2 t ground cinnamon
3/4 t ground ginger
1/4 t ground allspice
1 c dry white wine
2 T almond flour
1/3 c raisins or golden raisins
Flour, to dust the work surface
1 egg
1 recipe Hand Pie Dough (pg. 213)

1. First, prepare the leeks. Remove the root ends, then remove the tough dark leaves. Slice the leeks in half lengthwise and lay the flat sides on a cutting board. Then, cut into thin half-moons. Place the leeks in a medium

bowl full of water and stir them around two or three times with your hands, shaking loose any grit and dirt. Give the dirt a couple of minutes to settle at the bottom of the bowl, then scoop the leek slices from the top with your hands or a bird's nest strainer, being careful not to disturb the sediment. Drain the leeks on a paper towel and set aside.

2. Fill a small saucepan about 3/4 full with water and set over high heat. Add a tablespoon of salt to the water—you want it to be salty, because this is your chance to flavor the rutabaga. Remove the stem and root ends from the rutabaga, then peel. Cut the rutabaga into 1/2-inch dice, add the pieces to the boiling water in the pot, reduce the heat to a strong simmer, and cook until a fork just pierces the rutabaga, about 15–20 minutes. Drain the rutabagas in a colander and divide between two bowls. Mash the rutabagas in one of the bowls. Set both bowls aside.

3. Heat a large skillet over medium heat and add 1 1/2 T olive oil. Add the ground pork to the pan, breaking it into very small chunks. Cook, stirring occasionally, until the meat is cooked through and no pink remains. Line a plate with paper towels. Remove the meat from the pan and drain on the paper-lined plate. Set aside.

4. Wipe the skillet clean with a paper towel, then add the other 1 1/2 T olive oil to the pan. Return to medium heat, then add the leeks and chopped carrots. Cook until the vegetables begin to soften, about 5–8 minutes. Add the cinnamon, ginger, and allspice to the pan, stir to coat the vegetables, and cook until the spices warm and bloom, about 1–2 minutes more.

5. Add the white wine to the pan, bring to a boil, then reduce heat and cook down until it is reduced by half. Stir the almond flour into the pan.

6. Return the pork to the skillet. Add the mashed rutabagas and stir to combine all the ingredients thoroughly.

7. Fold the raisins and the rutabagas into the meat mixture. Remove from heat and allow to cool the filling to room temperature.

8. Remove the Hand Pie Dough disks from the refrigerator and set on the counter until they are at room temperature—they should be pliable and shouldn't crack when rolled. Line 2 baking sheets with parchment paper. Lightly scatter flour on your work surface and rolling pin.

9. Crack the egg in a small bowl. Add 3 T water and beat well.

10. Roll a pie dough disk into a circle about 6 inches in diameter. Spread 1/8 filling on the bottom of the dough circle, leaving a 1-inch border. Using a finger or the pastry brush, paint the egg wash onto the edge of the pastry dough. Fold the top half of the dough over the filling, pressing gently to release any air pockets—all you want is filling surrounded by two even layers of dough.

11. Using a fork dipped in a bit of flour, crimp the edges of the hand pie together. Place on the paper-lined baking sheet. Repeat with the other 7 pie disks, reserving the leftover egg wash.

12. Refrigerate the pies for one hour.

13. Preheat the oven to 400 degrees F.

14. When ready to bake, brush a thin layer of egg wash over the pies. Use a fork dipped in flour or a paring knife to create 2 or 3 air vents in each pie.

15. Place the baking pans in the oven, bake for 10 minutes, then reduce the temperature to 350 degrees. Bake until the pies are a deep golden brown and the internal temperature registers 165 degrees, about 30–40 minutes.
16. Using a spatula, remove the pies and set them on a cooling rack. Serve warm or at room temperature.

Hand Pie Dough

———

This is a simple but sturdy pastry dough. I like to imagine Erec and Enide stopping in between travels by a lovely stream in the Burgundian countryside, nibbling on pies provided by their last hosts, fortifying them for their next inevitable battle. Even if there is no jousting on the horizon, you'll find this easy dough perfect for any kind of turnover that will be packed in a picnic basket—or transported to book club. The sour cream makes it tender, and the butter assures there are lots of layers.

Equipment you will need: a rolling pin; parchment paper

Equipment that would be nice: a pastry blender

Yield: 8 hand pies

Ingredients:

2 c all-purpose flour, plus more for the work surface
1/4 t salt
8 T cold butter

3 T cold sour cream

8–12 T ice water

1. Whisk the flour and salt together in a large mixing bowl.
2. Remove the butter from the refrigerator. Working as quickly as possible, cut the butter into small pieces and scatter them over the flour mixture.
3. Using a pastry blender (or two knives pulled in opposite directions across the bowl if you don't have a pastry blender), cut the butter into the flour mixture until it resembles coarse crumbs, with no butter pieces being bigger than the size of a pea. Those pockets of butter will contribute to a flaky crust.
4. Add the sour cream to the flour mixture and cut into the flour mixture using the pastry blender until it is evenly distributed throughout. The dough will appear lumpy and resist holding together. Don't be tempted to overmix it.
5. Add the ice water to the mixture, 1 T at a time, and use a fork to blend it into the flour mixture. You want to add just enough water the hold the dough together—it's okay if there are still some crumbs visible.
6. Using your hand, knead the dough a few times in the bowl to make sure it holds together. If there are still a lot of crumbs, add another tablespoon of water and knead again.
7. Divide the dough into 8 pieces. Fashion each piece into a disk. Cover with plastic wrap and place in the refrigerator for at least 1 hour and up to 24 hours.

Herb and Cheese Fritters with Sour Fruit Sauce

We have never had the opportunity to learn from more amazing professional and home chefs. Television and social media bring the world's most creative food minds into our homes every day. I interact with food apps, podcasts, and hashtags daily, and there's no doubt I'm a better—and more adventurous—cook because of it.

While there are many kinds of foodies out there, the ones I gravitate toward are the ones who are good teachers. And I don't think there's a better teacher out there than French food baking expert Dorie Greenspan—author of numerous books, including *Dorie's Cookies* and *Baking with Dorie*. She has a way of explaining and contextualizing recipes that makes you excited to try them. But the best thing about her recipes is that they make you think. What else could I do with this?

What direction can I take this in? Could I make this savory instead of sweet? She's my foodie hero.

Medieval homes did not have ovens as a rule (bread dough was delivered to communal ovens and baked daily by professional bakers), but according to the comprehensive online index *Medieval Cookery,* cooks did turn out plenty of pancakes and fritters in skillets at home. Fritters are a great way to turn odds and ends into a tasty dinner, so I spent a lot of time testing recipes for them—when I remembered Dorie Greenspan's *farçous* recipe from *Around My French Table.* Her chard pancakes were a huge hit with my daughter, Eleanor, at a time when getting green things into her was not a simple prospect. And they had French "bona fides" to boot. But for a book club buffet, I wanted something more complex that could be enjoyed as a canape, so I knew I would need additions.

For herbs, I grabbed tarragon and thyme—I love how the floral and earthy notes complement each other. Because many of the fritter recipes I looked at included cheese, which adds tenderness to baked goods, I included some goat cheese. Added to a simple pancake batter, leavened only with frothy eggs, the pancakes were fantastic on their own. But made-up silver-dollar size, they made a perfect canape base. They were yummy with crème fraîche and a few nuts, and you can definitely go that way. But when I added a sour fruit sauce—vinegar was a common flavoring and preservative for both sweet and savory foods in the Middle Ages—a canape was born. Thanks for the inspiration, Dorie!

Equipment you will need: a Dutch oven; a non-stick frying pan or skillet

Equipment that would be nice: a food processor; a non-stick griddle

For the fruit sauce:

3 1/2 c chopped fruit (such as apples, pears, peaches, berries, or a combination)
1/4 c white wine
1 T honey
1/2 c chopped prunes
1 t salt
1/4 t ground cinnamon
1/4 t ground ginger
1/8 t ground cloves
2 t white wine vinegar

For the pancakes:

3 chard or Tuscan kale leaves, stems removed and roughly chopped
12 chives
3 sprigs fresh thyme, leaves removed
2 sprigs fresh tarragon, leaves removed
2 oz goat cheese
1 c all-purpose flour
1/2 t salt
1/4 t ground white pepper
2 eggs plus 1 egg white
1 c whole milk

Butter, for the pan
Crème fraîche (optional)
1/2 c walnuts, for garnish

1. For the sour fruit sauce: Add the chopped fruit, wine, and honey over medium heat in a Dutch oven or other heavy-bottomed pan. Bring to a boil.
2. Lower the heat and add chopped prunes, salt, and spices. Cover and simmer over low heat until the fruit is soft and the remaining liquid is thick and syrupy, about 30–40 minutes, depending on the fruits chosen. Add the vinegar and simmer another 3 minutes, uncovered. Remove from the heat.
3. For the pancakes: Place the chard and herbs in the bowl of a food processor. Pulse a few times until the leaves are finely cut but not totally pulverized (or pureed). Alternatively, using a sharp knife of a cutting board, cut the leaves into fine ribbons. Add the herbs to the board and run the knife over the greens a few times until they are finely minced. Set aside.
4. Remove the goat cheese from the refrigerator. Crumble the goat cheese into small pieces and add to the greens— this works better when the cheese is cold. Set aside.
5. In a separate bowl, whisk together the flour, salt, and white pepper. Set aside.
6. Measure the milk into a measuring cup. Add the 2 whole eggs, and whisk together (you can do this in a separate bowl if you wish),
7. In a medium bowl, whisk the egg white until it is frothy and opaque—this will give the pancakes some airiness.
8. Add the milk mixture to the flour mixture and whisk together until smooth. Stir in the greens and cheese to

distribute evenly. Gently fold in the egg whites, preserving as much air as possible—they'll deflate somewhat, but if you work fast, you'll preserve some of the air bubbles.

9. Bring a non-stick frying pan or an electric griddle to medium heat (about 300–325 degrees). Coat the surface with butter, then drop batter by tablespoons into the pan, leaving enough room for the pancakes to spread out a bit.

10. When the bubbles at the edge of the pancakes pop and remain open, and the bottoms of the pancakes are golden, use a spatula to flip them. Cook for another minute or so, until the bottoms are golden. Remove to a cooling rack. Continue, coating pan with butter as necessary, until all the batter is used.

11. In a non-stick skillet over low heat, gently toast the walnuts until they are lightly brown and you detect a warm, nutty aroma. Remove to a chopping board and allow to cool, then chop fine.

12. To serve, top each pancake with a bit of crème fraîche and some of the fruit sauce. Garnish with the toasted nuts and arrange the canapes on a serving platter.

Cornish Game Hens with Green Sauce

———

My favorite beach read is a cookbook. I love nothing more than immersing myself in a new cuisine or a new way of thinking about one with which I'm already familiar. Sitting by the ocean, imagining all the places I might go, is my favorite escape. So, it came as quite a shock when I started researching medieval cuisine for this book, and it felt surprisingly modern and familiar.

One of the best and most comprehensive takes on cooking in the Middle Ages is *Pleyn Delit: Medieval Cookery for Modern Cooks* by Constance Hieatt, Brenda Hosington, and Sharon Butler. The authors set out to recreate medieval recipes using current kitchen equipment and techniques. One thing that really stands out from reading their translated recipes is the sophistication of the cuisine. Before reading their book, I thought that the cuisine would be limited by the ovens of the time, and there are plenty of mentions of roasted meat, to be sure. But those seem to have been accompanied by a dizzying array of fresh, flavorful sauces that wouldn't be out of place in a Bobby Flay throwdown.

Another thing that surprised me was how healthy the food must have been by modern standards. The Catholic Church was the dominant institution of the time period, and its emphasis on fast days (days when all meat, dairy, and egg products were forbidden) and ember days (days when no meat products could be eaten, but dairy and eggs were allowed) led to a surprisingly plant-forward cuisine. So many sauces were thickened with ground nuts, adding protein and a healthy source of fat to a meal. (The other main thickener—day-old-bread—is in sync with another modern trend: reducing food waste. Everything old really is new again.)

Medieval cooks appear to have been "locavores." Recipes of the same name could be quite different based on where and at what time of year they were made. "Green Sauce," for example, is mentioned in a number of recipe compilations, but there is no consistency. Some use garlic; others do not. Some thicken with bread, while others use nuts, more like our ubiquitous "pesto." Liquids vary, though wine is often included. Some preparations are cooked, while others are raw—another current trend. So, when I put my own green sauce recipe together, I looked for ingredients easily found in any decently stocked American supermarket. To be true to the original, the sauce is on the thin side, adding a punch of flavor, but not real creaminess, to any dish it's paired with. But the herbs are flexible—you can change them with the seasons, or omit anything you don't like, and still get a taste of the times. And while almonds seemingly ruled the medieval table, other nuts such as hazelnuts, chestnuts, pine nuts, and walnuts appear in plenty of recipes. I think the assertive taste of walnuts stands up particularly well to the herbs in this green sauce. But you can certainly swap them out for another nut if you'd like.

I like to pair this green sauce with poultry, as it doesn't compete with the star attraction. "Utensils" during the medieval period were limited to two: a spoon and a knife. So, when planning a get-together with a medieval theme, it's fun to keep that in mind and try to imagine everything being eaten by hand. That's why Cornish game hens are so much fun on a medieval-inspired buffet table. They are easily spatchcocked for quick roasting, and half of a bird makes a perfect serving for one, daintily eaten by hand. (You can find plenty of videos demonstrating the process.) But the sauce would also be fantastic paired with white fish, such as cod or trout.

Since medieval meals consisted of many courses, and book clubs are made up of many types of eaters, a vegetarian or vegan accompaniment makes perfect sense. Rice is an obvious choice, as many medieval cooks made mention of it—but it was a very expensive imported food. Pasta would also be a sound choice. For a vegetable accompaniment true to the medieval era, don't look toward potatoes, which weren't introduced to Europe until the Renaissance. A puree of carrots, parsnips, or turnips might have been a contemporary choice. For a vegetarian main course, the sauce would also pair nicely with sautéed artichokes.

Yield: About 1 1/2 c sauce (enough for 6 servings)

Equipment you will need: a vegetable peeler; a food processor or blender (yes, you can grind it with a mortar and pestle to be truly authentic, but it's definitely not something I'd make time for); a boning knife

Equipment that would be nice: poultry shears; a lemon zester

Ingredients:

3 Cornish game hens (1 for every 2 people eating)
2 T olive oil
1/2 c chopped walnuts
1 preserved lemon
1 1/2 c packed flat parsley leaves (from 1 big bunch of parsley)
2 t snipped chives
8 mint leaves
24 basil leaves
1/4 t ground ginger
1/2 c dry white wine
1 T white wine vinegar
Water, as necessary
Salt and pepper to taste

1. Preheat oven to 400 degrees F.
2. First, spatchcock the Cornish game hens. Place the hen on a cutting board with the breast side down. Using a poultry shear or a sharp boning knife, cut the ribs close to the backbone on both sides, and remove them. (Backbones can be frozen and added to poultry stock later, if desired.) Open the hen like a book and turn it breast-side up on

the board. Using the heel of your hand, gently press down between the breast until the breastbone cracks—this will allow the hen to lay flat.

3. Line 2 rimmed baking sheets with parchment paper. Place the hens skin-side-up on the pans. Drizzle with olive oil, then season with salt and pepper. Rub in to distribute the oil and seasonings evenly.

4. Place the pans in the oven. If they do not fit on one rack, place one over the other and rotate front to back and upper to lower at 20 minutes.

5. Cook until an instant-read thermometer placed near the thigh joint registers 165 degrees F, about 50 minutes to 1 hour total.

6. While the hens are cooking, put the walnuts in a small, non-stick pan, over low heat. Toast them until they are golden brown and beginning to give off a deep, nutty aroma. Be careful not to burn any, as this will make the sauce bitter. Remove from the heat and place the nuts on a plate to cool.

7. Using a lemon zester or a vegetable peeler, carefully remove the skin from the preserved lemon. Work carefully, as you want to avoid the salty flesh underneath. Finely mince the lemon peel.

8. Add all the ingredients through the white wine vinegar to a food processor or blender and puree. If the puree is too thick, add water one tablespoon at a time until a smooth sauce that pours easily forms.

9. Taste for salt and pepper and adjust as necessary.

10. Using a kitchen shear, cut the hens in two. Arrange in one layer on a serving platter so skin remains crispy. Serve with the green sauce.

Saffron Bread Pudding

One thing I always do when I travel is ferreting out the spices that are essential to the cuisine. There's nothing like the thrill of finding a spice that's not easy to come by at home. During December of 2020, when most everyone was stuck in their houses because of social distancing, I came up with a virtual cook-along for a group of friends who usually enjoy getting together for some "fancy baking"—the kind of baking most of us home cooks do for big occasions—during the holidays. Because of the date (December 13) and my mother-in-law's partial Scandinavian ancestry, I chose St. Lucia buns, a sweet, yeasted bun scented with saffron traditionally made by the children of the house, who serve them while wearing a white gown and a crown of lighted candles. (Sure, that sounds like a recipe for disaster to me, but according to the *Why Christmas* site, children younger than twelve routinely use electric candles in their crowns, so I guess that's a good thing.) The morning of the cook-along, I had bags of yeast and saffron waiting at my front door, ready for friends who didn't have any on hand to pick up. But my friend Heather texted me to tell me that her partner was dropping something off instead.

After seeing the recipe, he wanted to share his stash of saffron from his family in Iran!

Honestly, I felt like Christmas had come early. The scent was more pungent and sweeter than my Spanish saffron. And the yellow color it turned the milk for the enriched dough was just heavenly. The buns were amazing, but my saffron mania didn't stop there. Armed with Mehrdad's tasty gift, I found myself using saffron all winter—in soups and stews, in savory dishes, and also in desserts. So, when I was trying to come up with an easy recipe for a book club inspired by medieval flavors, I knew I wanted to use saffron, a spice that had been re-introduced to the elite of Europe during the medieval era by the Moors.

Based on my research, reusing day-old bread was clearly a hallmark of medieval cookery. Since medieval chefs didn't distinguish sweet and savory courses, I hit on a not-too-sweet bread pudding; infused with saffron and sweetened with ripe fruit and honey. It's super simple and can be put together early in the day, or even the night before, then refrigerated, ready to bake up warm and fragrant right before it's needed. You could certainly focus on fruits of European origin if you want to stay authentic—red currants, figs, cherries, pears, apples, and plums would have been available. I don't worry about it too much, as I feel a medieval chef would have used what was good and handy. In summer, I make this pudding with a mix of berries and stone fruit, skipping the additional spices. But it's also wonderful with apples and pears in autumn, when the addition of cinnamon, mace, and ginger, so popular in the Middle Ages, now screams "holiday." In fact, this pudding would make an excellent and surprising addition to a Thanksgiving table.

Equipment you will need: a fine mesh strainer; a high sided cake pan or casserole pan; parchment paper; aluminum foil

Equipment that would be nice: an instant-read thermometer

Ingredients:

1 c heavy cream
1 c whole or 2% milk
1/2 c honey (*Miel de Provence* or lavender honey would be on point here, but any good honey will do)
1/2 tsp saffron threads
1 small round country or sourdough loaf (about 1 to 1 ¼ lbs)
4 eggs
1/2 t cinnamon (optional)
1/4 t mace (optional)
1/4 t dried ginger (optional)
2 c ripe fruit (berries, peaches, plums, cherries, grapes, figs, apples, pears—use what's ripe at the moment)
2 T butter, plus more for the pan

1. Set the cream, milk, and honey in a small saucepan over medium heat, bring to a heavy simmer, then remove from the heat. Add the saffron threads to the cream, cover the saucepan, and allow to steep for about an hour. The cream mixture should take on a nice yellow color and cool down to the temperature of a baby's bottle.
2. Meanwhile, dry the bread. Preheat the oven to 200 degrees F. Cut the bread into 2-inch cubes and place on a

large-rimmed baking tray, making sure the pieces do not overlap. Place the tray in the oven for about 30 minutes, removing the tray about halfway through the baking time to turn the bread over so it dries out more evenly. (You don't want it toasted, just dry so it can absorb the liquid). Remove the bread from the oven and set aside.

3. Pour the cream mixture through a fine mesh strainer into a large mixing bowl; discard the saffron threads.

4. Break the eggs into a small bowl and add them to the cream mixture one at a time. Add the dried spices, if using, and whisk thoroughly. Add the cooled bread to the cream and egg mixture, pushing it down with a rubber spatula and folding gently to make sure all the bread is soaked. At first, it might seem like you have too much liquid for the bread to absorb, but just give it some time.

5. When the liquid is mostly absorbed, gently fold the fruit into the bread mixture, making sure it is evenly distributed.

6. Preheat the oven to 325 degrees F. Butter the cake pan generously. Turn the bread mixture into the pan and gently press it down, making sure any unabsorbed liquid is scraped into the pan. Chop the butter into tiny pieces, and distribute evenly.

7. Cut a piece of parchment paper so that it just fits on the top of the pan. Gently press it onto the bread pudding mixture, then wrap the pan tightly with aluminum foil. Place in the center of the oven and allow to bake for 30 minutes.

8. After 30 minutes, remove the pan from the oven, carefully remove the foil and parchment paper, and return to the oven to bake for about 25–30 minutes more, until the top is browned, a knife inserted in the middle

comes out clean, and an instant-read thermometer reads 160 degrees F.

9. Serve hot, warm, or at room temperature. Ice cream was definitely not on the menu in medieval France, but if you happen to have a pint hanging around, it would be most fortuitous.

Taking Book Club to the Next Level: Erec and Enide

BEVERAGES TO OFFER:

Non-alcoholic drinks: Almond milk and hazelnut milk were staples of the many fast days during the era. Sure, you can make them yourself, but they're so readily available that it's a simple addition to your book club buffet. Equally authentic, but less easily obtainable in the US, is barley water, which is really a tisane of barley, water, sugar, or honey, and whatever other flavorings are handy. Medieval recipes refer to a variety of flavorings, including anise seeds and figs. Robinson's, a British brand of barley water, is available for delivery in the US from Amazon.

Alcoholic drinks: Wine is king when it comes to medieval beverages, and it would be my first choice. It was common to mull wine, warming it with cinnamon and other spices, such as in the famed Wassail Bowl, and mulled wine would be a fantastic idea for a winter meeting. No bubbly, though—champagne was perfected at a monastery, but Dom Perignon didn't taste those stars until the late seventeenth century.

In parts of France where viticulture was not widely practiced, beer would have been widely available. Medieval monks were brewers as well as winemakers, so an abbey beer would be particularly appropriate. St. Joseph's Abbey near Boston is the home to Spencer Brewery, the only Trappist brewery in the US, but it's not easy to get their ale because of the relatively small batches the monks turn out. Chimay, a Trappist ale from Belgium, is more widely available in the US. Many local craft breweries make "abbey-style" ales, which tend to be sweeter, fruitier, and more alcoholic than other ales. They'd fit right in at book club and would allow you to support a local business as well.

MUSIC TO PLAY/VIDEOS TO STREAM:

There's plenty of interest in historical music, and streaming services have scads of choices you can find by simply searching for "medieval music." There are a few artists who specialize in the genre, both vocalists and instrumental. But there are also quite a few contemporary movie soundtracks, such as that of the *Witcher* series, that feature period music stylized in the way we all *think* it sounds.

I couldn't find a movie version of *Erec and Enide*—not even in French, with subtitles. Kind of surprising for a story that's been told and retold for close to a thousand years. So, if your book club wants to include a movie, you'd have to look to one of the bazillion movies featuring Arthur and the Knights of the Round Table.

WHAT TO BRING/TABLESCAPES:

Happily, sourdough bread has a seat at the medieval table, so go ahead and include a few loaves. Since medieval cooks would have turned to the garden in summer, a simple green salad picked up from your grocery store's salad bar would be a suitable accompaniment. And finally, to replicate the spicy/sour/sweet combination so popular during the period, you could easily include a jar of chutney on the table.

When it comes to the table, put the forks away! Medieval diners would have used a spoon and a knife to eat their food, along with their fingers. Since guests generally brought their own utensils, you could do the same—just be careful driving if you choose to hang your knife from your belt as they would have in the twelfth century. A medieval meal would have been served on a trencher, basically a stale round of bread. You can find directions on the Internet for making your own trenchers, but that honestly sounds a bit crazy to me. If you want to recreate the concept without the schlep, just serve one of the recipes in this section on a thick piece of toast!

Epilogue: The Little Women Crash the Party, or Better Understanding Through Books

——

Being a pretty basic cook didn't keep my mom from being a fantastic party thrower. My dad was the cornerstone of a vast and incredibly diverse group of friends, many of whom had been together since their PS 12* days in Queens back in the early 1940s. The "Woodside Crowd" started out playing baseball together in the schoolyard, went into the military around the same time, then attended each other's weddings, and acted as godparents and confirmation sponsors for each other's children. And beginning in the early 1960s, where the Woodside Crew went, a raucous, alcohol-fueled party usually followed, often spearheaded by Moe, my redheaded dynamo of a mother.

Parties at our house in the 1960s and 70s routinely included a cast of cops, secretaries, teachers, lawyers, and railroad engineers, as well as many stay-at-home moms like mine. But of all the Woodside Crowd, my favorite couple was Billy and Jo McMahon, the liberal, pot-smoking, hippie fringe of the assemblage. In addition to being a superb shortstop, Billy was a sculptor of some renown. And his wife, Jo, was a children's book illustrator. They lived in a loft in the flower district of New York City, and Jo maintained a roof garden above it that I thought was the most magical place in the world: rows of vegetables growing in pots, vines hanging from wires, secret spaces for reading while the traffic honked below on the street. Billy and Jo were the only people I knew who didn't own a car. My brothers and I would jump up and down, trying to be the first to spot them as their train pulled into the picturesque St. James Railroad Station on their way to one of my mom's shindigs.

On the day of one of her parties, my mother went into Commander mode, directing cleaning and provisioning activities with the strategic acumen of a seasoned campaign veteran. "Peel the potatoes as soon as they've cooled down, or the potato salad won't be ready on time." "I don't think we have enough ice. Quick, run to the store for a few more bags!" The portable bar would emerge like clockwork from the basement to be stocked with gin, scotch, rye, and whatever else people were drinking then. (I remember the Melon Ball year being particularly calamitous for the shag carpet.) There was a big cooler for beer and sodas. Food was not the thing at those parties, although there was plenty of it. Terry would bring a spinach-artichoke dip; Sarah brought pastries from her favorite bakery. But it wasn't something my mom stressed about. As long as everyone was together, it was going to be a great time, even if she served warmed-up White Castle hamburgers—which my mom did one year, to the collective euphoria of the Queens denizens deprived of them when they'd moved their families to "The Island."

In advance of the party, my brothers and I were assigned age-appropriate duties: dusting the den, trimming the bread crusts to make pinwheels, setting the tables. But my parents' parties weren't family events. We Connolly kids knew our role was to help get everything ready, make one polite pass with the hors d'oeuvres, kiss all the "aunts" and "uncles" goodnight, and then head upstairs to our bedrooms without complaint. Kind of like the von Trapp children, but without the matching outfits and the high production value.

That was usually fine with me because, while the party bubbled along, no one was monitoring bedtime, which meant I got extra time with whatever book I was devouring. During my parents' annual Christmas party in 1974, I was deep into Louisa Mae Alcott's *Little Women*. I adored all the March sisters as only a girl with two brothers can. I knew if I had a sister, I'd be the "Jo" in the mix, adventurous and going places girls didn't usually go. I thought Meg was a bit prim and boring (although she wound up being closest to my personality in the end), and I was annoyed by bratty Amy (who isn't?). But Beth had my heart. She was so sweet and so kind—who doesn't want someone like that in their life? She was the endlessly patient, adoring sister of my dreams.

So, on that evening, as the Christmas cheer steadily increased downstairs, I was starting to get really worried. Jo had taken Beth to the seashore, but her health didn't seem to be improving. Jo seemed to accept that Beth wasn't going to get better, which had me pretty confused—she didn't seem like the type to give up. Meg was learning how to be a good wife (yawn), Amy was being annoying somewhere in France (eye roll), and then I got to Chapter Forty, "The Valley of the Shadow." I was Catholic enough to know that didn't sound good. But I was still pretty sure there was a miracle cure on the way. I read on. And then, finally, it happened: Beth "quietly drew her last, with no farewell but one loving look, one little sigh."

And I started to cry.

Not a little bit. Not some reverential tears falling down my cheek. I lost it. I was crying so hard I could hardly catch my breath. I couldn't calm myself down. My own reaction frightened me so much that I committed the ultimate crime—I went running down the stairs during a grown-up party.

The first person to see me by the staircase was my Uncle Al, a giant mountain of a guy with a handlebar mustache and a scary, gravelly voice. He seemed tough, but any kid in the room figured out he was a total pushover in about three seconds. He appeared genuinely alarmed and brought me quickly to my dad. My dad was tending bar, handing someone a drink, when he caught sight of Al and promptly came to us.

"Witch, what's wrong?" Oddly, perhaps, a term of endearment in our household.

I could only gasp.

"Colleen, you need to calm yourself down and let me know what's going on." His cop voice.

I tried to speak. Another sob escaped. I clung to him, still shaking.

"Colleen Mariah Connolly, what happened?" Mom had entered the living room.

She'd used my full name. I gasped, which actually allowed some air into my lungs.

"Beth died!" That was all I could get out.

The party got really quiet at that. My dad patted my head and looked toward my mom. "Who's Beth?"

I could see my mom wracking her brain for an answer, going through the mental Rolodex of my friends, coming up with nothing. I knew I needed to explain, but I was still sobbing, now anxious about ruining the party in addition to losing a beloved character. And then I felt a hand on my shoulder. And a gentle voice asked, "Colleen, sweetheart, are you reading *Little Women*?" It was my *own* Jo, Jo McMahon, a person who loved books so much she turned them into pictures. Of course.

In the face of perfect understanding, I was finally able to breathe. I nodded furiously. "Uh-huh!"

My dad was still bewildered. "It's okay, Mike. Beth died right after the Civil War." I guess there was a collective sigh of relief. Probably a few laughs. And then the party started up again.

"This was all over a *book*?"

"Of course. Colleen and I are going to go upstairs and talk about it now." The quietest member of the Woodside Crowd just smiled at my astonished parents. Then she took my hand and led me upstairs and sat on my bed for quite a while, discussing things such as whether or not Alcott could have written it any other way or why the bratty Amy wasn't the one to go, along with a whole bunch of other things I don't remember. I do remember she begged me to finish the book, even though I was disappointed. Then, after telling me to head to bed, she returned to the party, which had gotten back to its regular buzz. I fell asleep listening to the sounds of long-term friendship and Frank Sinatra singing carols. And the next day, despite a gut reaction to throw it in the garbage, I finished *Little Women*. Maybe it wasn't the ending I would have written, but I realized all the characters wound up exactly where Alcott thought they should be. And I realized that was perfect.

I think that's when I realized how books are so much more than personal. Sharing books can build understanding, and community, and even life-long friendships. Every time I give someone a book recommendation or see a story from a different point of view because I'm discussing it with a friend, I still think of Jo McMahon and that crazy Christmas party. And I know that nothing is better than friends who share a love of books—which is one of the best reasons for making time for book club.

*Note: That's Public School Number 12 in New York-ese.

Acknowledgements

Some version of this book has been rattling around in my head for years. Getting to the part where I'm finally writing the Acknowledgements is the result of so much support, goodwill, and flat-out kindness that I'm kind of bewildered to find myself here. Anyone mentioned in this section can be assured of a home-cooked meal the next time they find themselves in State College, PA, or Corolla, NC—whether I have a working oven or not.

Thanks, Anne Hoag, for off-handedly suggesting we take on a book writing project together. Just knowing you were on the other side of the Zoom call made the tomato writing a little bit easier. I can't wait to get your book, *Knitting Entrepreneurship*, into my hands.

Thanks, Eric Koester, for inviting me to join the Book Creators community. You've created a system that takes a pretty decent idea and turns it into words on pages. It's good to be reminded how much difference an enthusiastic teacher can make in someone's life.

Thanks to the fantastic team at New Degree Press. People always thank their publishers in the Acknowledge-ments, but until I went through the process, I didn't under-stand why. New Degree's author-centered press model gave me the tools to get this to the finish line. Special thanks to Megan Hennessey, my DE, who challenged me to make this manuscript more than I imagined in her typically Socratic way; this book evolved considerably because of her questions and insights. And to Olivia Bearden, my MRE, who kept track of my progress, pushed just enough, and didn't let me throw in the towel when I was *so close.*

Thanks to the people who believed so much in this project that they bought their copies before it was even done! Not wanting to disappoint you all was the reason I sat down and wrote a few paragraphs some days. I truly hope you enjoy the book you helped make a reality, Abigail Ahern, Elea-nor Ahern, Christopher and Orellana Bandera, Madeleine J. Bandera, Denise Bortree, Lois Boynton, Courtney Bree, S. Camille Broadway, Joanne Fago, Julia Daisy Fraustino, San-dra Friedrich, Ebru Gurun, Anne Hoag, Suzanne Horsley, Cheryl Howard, Carrie Ann Johnson, Amanda Koch, Eric Koester, Sarah Kollat, Ellen Lambert, Stephanie Madden, Karen Magri, Wendy Margetis, Nadia Martinez, Deanna Nagle, Christine O'Neil, Valerie Ord, Louise Page, Shaheen Pasha, Jessica Ruiz, Karen Russell, Amy Sauertieg, Lauren Schroeder, Maura Shea, Heather Shoenberger, Akshaya Sreenivasan, Jessica Stern, Hunter Thomas, David Weiss, Rachel Wolkenhauer, Tara Wyckoff, and Doreen Zilli!

This book idea started to crystallize when I gave a Nerd Nite talk on why I love matching books and food, focused on my favorite novel, *Pride and Prejudice*. Thanks to Stephanie Madden (there's another one) for suggesting I participate in Nerd Nite, and Elaine Wilgus of Webster's Book Store in State College, PA, for hosting Nerd Nite, as well as so many other community events.

Two groups of women have been a source of unfailing support, cheer, and occasional snarkiness (but only when absolutely necessary) while I was working on this project. Thanks to the PR Divas, who always tell it like it is, and especially to Pat Curtin, who started the thread. And thanks to the Badass Book Bitches, founded by Stephanie Madden (there she is again), a book club more about women and empowerment than actual reading, which is just fine by me.

Thanks to my big, loud, extended family—so many things I love about food were from hanging around with you all after dinner. Special thanks to my Auntie Jo-Jo, who's always there to listen, and my cousin, Christine O'Neil, for sharing her home and ingredients so generously while I worked on this manuscript.

Thanks to Kay Ahern and Sandy Friedrich, who tested recipes for me and gave me thoughtful feedback about ingredient availability and my version of "spicy."

My daughters are my biggest cheerleaders (and book promoters, apparently). Thanks, Abigail and Eleanor. I've said it a million times, but I love having adult daughters. Thanks for a lifetime of taste-testing and recipe-testing. Thanks for every card, call, and text. But mostly, thanks for continuing to share your lives with me every day. You are, quite simply, my joy.

And, finally, thanks to Lee, my best friend, husband, and erstwhile photographer. You must be magic, Lee sweetie, because when I dream my crazy dreams, you somehow find a way to make them come true. Just no more projects for a while, okay?

Works Referenced

—

KOREA

10 Magazine Staff. (2019, May 26). A Taste of Korea: When Barley Met Rice Boribap. *10 Magazine*. Retrieved October 21, 2021, from https://10mag.com/taste-korea-boribab/

Deuchler, M. (1980). Neo-Confucianism: The Impulse for Social Action in Early Yi Korea. *The Journal of Korean Studies, 2,* 71-111. Retrieved June 1, 2021, from http://www.jstor.org/stable/41490153

Ford, H.K. (2021). Beyond kimchee. Retrieved June 20, 2021, from https://www.beyondkimchee.com/

Ford, H.K. *Korean Cooking Favorites: Kimchi, BBQ, Bibimbap and So Much More.* Boston: Page Street Publishing.

Hahm H. (2016) Rice in Korea. In: Selin H. (eds) *Encyclopaedia of the History of Science, Technology, and Medicine in Non-Western Cultures.* Springer, Dordrecht. doi.org/10.1007/978-94-007-7747-7_10280

Hatchett, C. (2020, October 14). Get to Know Makgeolli, Korea's Ancient Rice Beverage. Liquor.com. Retrieved June 20, 2021, from https://www.liquor.com/makgeolli-5082294

Hempinstall, H.S.S. (2001). *Growing Up in a Korean Kitchen: A Cookbook.* Berkley, California: Ten Speed Press.

Hong, D., & Rodbard, M. (2016). *Koreatown: A Cookbook.* New York: Clarkson Potter/Publishers.

Instrok.org. (2007). The Cultural Values of the Choson Dynasty. *The Wayback Machine*: https://web.archive.org/web/20070928110156/http://www.instrok.org/instrok/lesson1/page03.html?thisChar=6

Kim, K. (1996). *An Introduction to Classical Korean Literature: From Hyangga to P'ansori.* Armonk, NY: M.E. Sharpe.

Kim S. H. (2007). Cultural perspectives and current consumption changes of cooked rice in Korean diet. *Nutrition Research and Practice, 1*(1), 8–13. https://doi.org/10.4162/nrp.2007.1.1.8

Kim, S.H., Kim, S.M., Lee, M.S., Park, Y.S., Lee, J.H., Kang, S., . . . Kwon, D.Y. (2016, Mar). Korean diet: Characteristics and historical background. *Journal of Ethnic Foods, 3*(1), 26-31. Retrieved from https://doi.org/10.1016/j.jef.2016.03.002

Maangchi, & Shulman, M.R. (2019). *Maangchi's Big Book of Korean Cooking: From Everyday Meals to Celebration Cuisine.* New York: Mariner Books.

Shin, J. (2016). *The Tale of Chun Hyang* (C.R. Chul, Trans.). New York: Olympia Press.

REGENCY ENGLAND

Austen, J. (2017) *Pride and Prejudice*. Kindle e-books. Seattle, WA: AmazonClassics.

Flood, A. (2021, 17 May). Want to Try Jane Austen's Favorite Cheese Toastie? Now You Can. *The Guardian*. Retrieved October 20, 2021, https://www.theguardian.com/books/2021/may/17/want-to-try-jane-austens-favourite-cheese-toastie-now-you-can

Grossman, A.C., & Thomas, L.G. (1997. *Lobscouse & Spotted Dog: Which It's a Gastronomic Companion to the Aubrey/Maturin Novels*. New York: W.W. Norton & Company.

Hughes, G. (2020, Nov 11). The Foods of England Project at http://www.foodsofengland.co.uk/

Hughes, G. (2017). *The Lost Foods of England*. Derbyshire, UK: Lulu.com

Rylance, R. (2012). *The Epicure's Almanack: Eating and Drinking in Regency London (The Original 1815 Guidebook)*. London: British Library.

Vogler, P. (2013, 21 Nov.) Pride and Partridges: Jane Austen and Food. *The Guardian*. Retrieved October 20, 2021, from https://www.theguardian.com/books/2013/nov/21/jane-austen-food-emma-bennet-dining

SPAIN

Burgen, S. (2021, Feb 23). 'A role model': How Seville is Turning Leftover Oranges into Electricity. *The Guardian.* Retrieved October 21, 2021, from https://www.theguardian.com/environment/2021/feb/23/how-seville-is-turning-leftover-oranges-into-electricity

Casas, P. (2005). *La Cocina de Mama: The Great Home Cooking of Spain.* New York: Broadway Books.

Chamberlin, V.A., & Hardin, V.F. Pepita Jiménez and the Romance tradition. Kansas University Scholar Works. Retrieved October 22, 2021, from https://kuscholarworks.ku.edu/bitstream/handle/1808/24278/chamberlin_1990_pepita.pdf?sequence=1&isAllowed=y

De la Escosura, L.P., & Caballero, C.S. and Carlos Santiago-Caballero. (2018, May 29). The Napoleonic Wars: A watershed in Spanish History?" The NEP-HIS Blog. Retrieved October 21, 2021, from https://nephist.wordpress.com/2018/05/29/the-economic-consequences-of-the-napoleonic-wars/

Madland, H. (1980). Time in Pepita Jiménez. *Romance Notes, 21*(2), 169-173. Retrieved June 24, 2021, from http://www.jstor.org/stable/43801690

Sevilla, M.J. (2019). Delicioso: A Food History of Spain. London: Reaktion Books Ltd.

Spanish Books. (2011) *Life and Works of Juan Valera.* Retrieved October 12, 2021, from https://www.classicspanishbooks.com/19th-cent-realism-prose-juan-valera.html

Valera, J. (2015). *Pepita Jiménez: Bilingual Edition*. Seattle, WA: Kindle.

Weldon Owen Inc. and Williams-Sonoma. (2004). *Barcelona*. Menlo Park, CA: Oxmoor House.

MEDIEVAL FRANCE

Carrol, M.P. (2021). *The Cult of the Virgin Mary: Psychological Origins*. Princeton, NJ: Princeton University Press.

Catholic Culture. (2021). Catholic Recipes for the Liturgical Year. Retrieved October 2, 2021, from https://www.catholicculture. org/culture/liturgicalyear/recipes/index.cfm

Clarkson, J. (2009). *Pies: A Global History*. London: Reaktion Books Ltd.

De Troyes, C. (2018). Erec and Enide (A.S. Kline, Trans.). Open Access: Poetry in Translation.

Department of English. (2000, Aug 17). Courtly love. *Brooklyn College CUNY*. Retrieved October 21, 2021, from http://academic. brooklyn.cuny.edu/english/melani/cs6/love.html

Department of Medieval Art and The Cloisters. (2000). The Cult of the Virgin Mary in the Middle Ages *The Metropolitan Museum of Art*. Retrieved October 21, 2021, from http://www.metmuseum.org/toah/hd/virg/hd_virg.htm (October 2001)

Duby, G. (1992). *France in the Middle Ages 987-1460*. Oxford, UK: Wiley-Blackwell.

Frost, N. (2017, July 27). How Medieval Chefs Tackled Meat-Free Days. Atlas Obscura. Retrieved October 21, 2021, from https://www.atlasobscura.com/articles/mock-medieval-foods

Greenspan, D. (2010). Around My French Table: More Than 300 Recipes from My Home to Yours. Boston: Houghton Mifflin Harcourt.

Hieatt, C.B., Hosington, B., & Butler, S. (1997). *Pleyn Delit: Medieval Cookery for Modern Cooks* (2nd ed.). Toronto: University of Toronto Press.

Lyon, K. (2015, Dec 4). The Four Humors: Eating in the Renaissance. *Shakespeare & Beyond*. Retrieved October 2, 2021, from https://shakespeareandbeyond.folger.edu/2015/12/04/the-four-humors-eating-in-the-renaissance/.

Medieval Cookery Database. *Medieval Cookery*. Retrieved October 20, 2021, from http://www.medievalcookery.com/

Miller, M. (2020, Apr 7). How to Make a Medieval Trencher. *Tasting History*. Retrieved October 5, 2021, from https://www.youtube.com/watch?v=rQT-aY9sTCI

Moncorge, M.J. (2021). Spices in Medieval Europe. *Old Cooks*. Retrieved October 4, 2021, from https://www.oldcook.com/en/medieval-spices

Moretti, S. (2019, Sep 8). How Monks Perfected Beer and Found Salvation in the Blessings of Liquid Bread. Medium. Retrieved October 21, 2021, from https://medium.com/a-brief-history-of-things/how-monks-perfected-beer-5cf78fc66022#:~:-

text=They%20also%20made%20other%20brewing,5%25%20
alcohol%2C%20to%20travelers.&text=Fast%20forward%20
almost%20600%20years,the%20best%20in%20the%20world

National Institutes of Health. (2013, Sept 19). The world of Shakespeare's humors. Retrieved October 19, 2021, from https://www.nlm.nih.gov/exhibition/shakespeare/fourhumors.html

Second Bottle. (n.d.) Monk Wine: The Role of Monks in Winemaking. Retrieved October 21, 2021, from https://www.catholicculture.org/culture/liturgicalyear/recipes/index.cfm

Selman, R. (2014, Jan 26). The Middle Ages: From Fasting to Feasting. *From Page to Plate.* Retrieved October 21, 2021, from http://frompagetoplate.com/2014/01/26/the-middle-ages-from-fasting-to-feasting/

Spengler, R.N. III (2021, 5 Jan). The Silk Road Origins of the Food We Eat. UC Press Blog. Retrieved October 19, 2021, from https://www.ucpress.edu/blog/45550/the-silk-road-origins-of-the-foods-we-eat/

Straw, K. (2013, Jan 21). The History of Utensils. *Gourmet Gift Baskets.com.* Retrieved October 20, 2021, from https://www.gourmetgiftbaskets.com/Blog/post/the-history-of-utensils.aspx#:~:text=In%20the%20Middle%20Ages%2C%20hosts,eating%20directly%20off%20the%20knife.

Tebben, M. (2020). *Savoir-faire: A History of Food in France.* London: Reaktion Books Ltd.

Weir, A. (2001). *Eleanor of Aquitaine.* New York: Ballantine Books.

Wright, K. (2021). Jance Sauce. *The Common Place Book of Lady Avelyn Grene.* Retrieved October 20, 2021, from http://grene-boke.com/recipes/jancesauce.html

CPSIA information can be obtained
at www.ICGtesting.com
Printed in the USA
LVHW050010190422
716535LV00012B/1847